Elements of **Language**

Developmental Language Skills

- Grammar
- Usage
- Mechanics

HOLT, RINEHART AND WINSTON

A Harcourt Education Company

Orlando • **Austin** • New York • San Diego • London

ISBN 978-0-03-099195-0
ISBN 0-03-099195-1

2 3 4 5 6   018   13 12 11 10 09 08

Contents

Contents

Using This Workbook

The worksheets in this workbook provide additional instruction, practice, and reinforcement for *Elements of Language* and *Language Skills Practice.*

This workbook is designed to supplement *Language Skills Practice* by providing additional instruction and practice to students who have not yet mastered the rules and topics covered in *Elements of Language.*

You will find throughout the workbook several special features, which have been added to aid students' mastery of grammar, usage, and mechanics. The special features include notes, reminders, tips, points of instruction after instructional and exercise examples, and guided practice for the first one or two items in each exercise.

- **Notes** provide students with pertinent information related to the rule or topic covered on a given worksheet.

- **Reminders** review grammatical terms and concepts that were covered on previous worksheets.

- **Tips** provide students with tangible aids for understanding abstract concepts. These tips include mnemonic devices, identification tests, and recognition strategies.

- **Points of Instruction** explain how the rule or topic applies to the instructional and exercise examples provided.

- **Guided Practice** helps students with the first one or two items of each exercise by asking questions that guide students to the correct answer.

Teacher's Notes and an **Answer Key** are provided on the *Teacher One Stop*™ **DVD-ROM with ExamView® Test Generator**.

v

Symbols for Revising and Proofreading

Symbol	Example	Meaning of Symbol
≡	at Scott lake	Capitalize a lowercase letter.
/	a gift for my Uncle	Lowercase a capital letter.
∧	cost *fifty* cents	Insert a missing word, letter, or punctuation mark.
⌐	by ~~their~~ *our* house	Replace something.
℘	What day is is it?	Leave out a word, letter, or punctuation mark.
⊓	recieved	Change the order of letters or words.
¶	¶The last step is	Begin a new paragraph.
⊙	Please be patient.	Add a period.
∧	Yes that's right.	Add a comma.

Sentences and Sentence Fragments

1a. A *sentence* is a word group that contains a subject and a verb and that expresses a complete thought.

When we say that a sentence expresses a complete thought, we mean that the sentence can stand alone. A sentence also begins with a capital letter and ends with a period, a question mark, or an exclamation point.

EXAMPLES **B**ianca finished her chores quickly. [The subject is *Bianca,* and the verb is *finished*. This word group expresses a complete thought.]

Have you met my cousin yet**?** [The subject is *you,* and the verb is *Have met.* This word group expresses a complete thought.]

Please watch your step**!** [The subject *you* is understood. The verb is *watch*. This word group expresses a complete thought.]

EXERCISE A Add capital letters and end marks to the following word groups to make them sentences. Write your answers on the lines provided.

Example 1. this postcard was sent from Arizona [Adding a capital letter at the beginning and a period at the end will make this word group a sentence.]

This postcard was sent from Arizona.

1. when will the next train leave [Which word begins the sentence? What end mark is appropriate?]

____

2. the class planted ten new trees

____

3. look at those stars

____

4. what a wonderful play that was

____

5. has my letter arrived yet

____

A *sentence fragment* is a group of words that looks like a sentence but does not contain both a subject and a verb or does not express a complete thought. Sentence fragments are common in conversation but are generally not appropriate in formal writing or speaking.

SENTENCE FRAGMENT Works three nights per week. [The word group has a verb, *Works,* but it does not have a subject.]

SENTENCE Carlton works three nights per week. [The word group has a subject, *Carlton,* and a verb, *works.*]

Developmental Language Skills

> **SENTENCE FRAGMENT**   After the bell rings. [The word group has a subject, *bell,* and a verb, *rings,* but it does not express a complete thought.]
>
> **SENTENCE**   You can talk to the teacher after the bell rings. [The word group *You can talk to the teacher* has a subject, *You,* and a verb, *can talk,* and expresses a complete thought. The word group *after the bell rings* is added to a word group that does express a complete thought.]

EXERCISE B On the line provided, write *S* if the word group is a sentence or *F* if the word group is a sentence fragment.

Example __*F*__ **1.** When the water is hot. [This word group has a subject, *water,* and a verb, *is.*

   However, the word group does not express a complete thought.]

_______ **6.** Went through the door. [Does this word group express a complete thought?]

_______ **7.** The substitute teacher in English class.

_______ **8.** Squirrels had buried acorns beneath the tree.

_______ **9.** Connie joined the volleyball team.

_______ **10.** Saw whom?

EXERCISE C The following items are sentence fragments. Add words to make each fragment a complete sentence. Write your answers on the lines provided.

Example 1. When the rain stops. [This word group has a subject, *rain,* and a verb, *stops.* However, the

   word group does not express a complete thought, so it is a sentence fragment. The

   revised sentence has a subject and a verb and expresses a complete thought.]

   When the rain stops, please take the dog for a walk. _______________________

11. Sent an e-mail to her cousin. [Does the word group need a subject or a verb?]

____

12. After the car has been washed.

____

13. Threw a long touchdown pass.

____

14. A terrific writer!

____

15. What the final score?

____

The Subject

Subjects

Every sentence has two basic parts: the subject and the predicate.

1b. The **subject** tells *whom* or *what* the sentence is about.

> **EXAMPLES** **Hank Aaron** was a magnificent baseball player. [*Hank Aaron* is *who* the sentence is about.]
>
> **His record of 755 home runs** was set on July 20, 1976. [*His record of 755 home runs* is *what* the sentence is about.]

You may find the subject at the beginning, in the middle, or at the end of the sentence.

> **EXAMPLES** **Mike** will be first at bat.
>
> Behind the baseball diamond, **the stands** are packed with fans.
>
> In the outfield is **our best catcher.**

EXERCISE A Underline the subject in each of the following sentences.

Example 1. Inside the book was <u>a map of the solar system</u>. [What was inside the book? A map of the solar system was.]

1. Throughout the solar system are eight planets. [What are throughout the solar system?]

2. Just before sunrise and just after sunset, planets are visible.

3. With a telescope, you can see Saturn's rings.

4. Pictures of the Martian landscape may amaze you.

5. Two satellites orbit the planet Mars.

Complete Subjects and Simple Subjects

The **complete subject** of a sentence consists of all the words needed to tell whom or what the sentence is about. The **simple subject** is part of the complete subject.

1c. The **simple subject** is the main word or word group that tells *whom* or *what* the sentence is about.

> **EXAMPLES** The crisp, white **curtains** fluttered in the breeze. [The complete subject is *The crisp, white curtains,* and the simple subject is *curtains.*]
>
> Are Vickie's **friends** from school making her a birthday card? [The complete subject is *Vickie's friends from school,* and the simple subject is *friends.*]

GO ON ➡

Sometimes the same word or word group makes up both the simple subject and the complete subject.

> **EXAMPLE** In the garden, **Aunt Clara** pulled many weeds. [*Aunt Clara* is the complete subject. It is also the simple subject.]

EXERCISE B Underline the complete subject once in each of the following sentences. Then, draw a second line under the simple subject.

Example 1. A basket of peaches sat upon the orchard wall. [*A basket of peaches* tells what the sentence is about. The main word in the complete subject is *basket*.]

6. Many colorful balloons floated above the dance floor. [Which words tell what the sentence is about? What is the main word in the complete subject?]

7. When are the Connors moving to Arizona?

8. Dust covered the furniture in the old house.

9. Above the sofa in the den hangs a painting of a country landscape.

10. Did you speak to Evan about our plans for tonight?

Compound Subjects

| **1f.** | A ***compound subject*** consists of two or more subjects that are joined by a connecting word and that have the same verb. |

The parts of a compound subject are usually connected by *and* or *or*.

> **EXAMPLE** **Mushrooms, broccoli,** or **onions** would taste good on your potato.
> [*Mushrooms, broccoli,* and *onions* are the three parts of the compound subject. They have the same verb, *would taste*.]

EXERCISE C Underline each part of the compound subject in the following sentences. Hint: Do not underline the connecting word that joins the parts of the compound subject.

Example 1. Several basketballs, some volleyballs, and nets are stored in the gym. [*Basketballs, volleyballs,* and *nets* make up the compound subject of the verb *are stored*.]

11. Noel and Kendall are starring in the play. [Which words make up the compound subject of the verb *are starring*?]

12. Sweaters or jackets are on sale this week.

13. Are maps, dictionaries, and encyclopedias in the reference section?

14. Under the rug were dust and dirt.

15. During the open house, parents and relatives viewed the students' work.

4   Introductory Course

The Predicate

Predicates

Every sentence has two basic parts: the subject and the predicate.

1d. The ***predicate*** of a sentence tells something about the subject.

> **EXAMPLES** Tomasina **recycles paper and plastic.** [The predicate tells something about the subject, Tomasina.]
>
> **Was** the friendly dragon **named Scaly?** [The predicate tells something about the subject, the friendly dragon.]

EXERCISE A Underline the predicate in each of the following sentences.

Example 1. Brandon was eating cereal for breakfast. [*Was eating cereal for breakfast* tells something about Brandon.]

1. The crunchy cereal suddenly popped! [What words tell something about the crunchy cereal?]

2. Each piece of cereal contained starch.

3. Inside the starch were air pockets.

4. In the milk, the starch became wet.

5. The air pockets then exploded with a pop.

Complete Predicates and Simple Predicates

The ***complete predicate*** consists of a verb and all the words that describe the verb and complete its meaning. The predicate usually comes after the subject. Sometimes, however, part or all of the predicate comes before the subject.

> **EXAMPLES** **Carefully,** Sandra **worked the math problem.** [Part of the predicate, *Carefully,* comes before the subject.]
>
> **Beneath the surface swam** goldfish. [All of the predicate comes before the subject.]

1e. The ***simple predicate,*** or ***verb,*** is the main word or word group in the complete predicate.

> **EXAMPLES** Fran **mailed** the birthday card. [*Mailed the birthday card* tells something about Fran. The main word in the complete predicate is *mailed.*]
>
> Liang **has kicked** the ball through the goal! [*Has kicked the ball through the goal* tells something about Liang. The main word group in the complete predicate is *has kicked.*]

The simple predicate may be a single verb or a ***verb phrase.*** A verb phrase is a verb with one or more helping verbs.

> **EXAMPLES** Glenn **practiced** his solo. [single verb]
>
> **Has** he **been practicing** for half an hour? [verb phrase]

GO ON ➡

NOTE The words *not* and *never* and the contraction *–n't* are not verbs. In the sentence *Cheryl wasn't happy,* the verb is *was.* The contraction *n't* is not part of the verb.

EXERCISE B Underline the complete predicate once in each of the following sentences. Then, draw a second line under the simple predicate (the verb). Hint: Remember that *not, n't,* and *never* are not verbs.

Example 1. Was a secret room behind the wall? [*Was behind the wall* asks something about a secret

room. *Was* is the main word in the complete predicate.]

6. Katie reads books about science fiction and adventure. [Which words tell something about Katie?

Which word is the main word in the complete predicate?]

7. Michelle has never been a judge for the art contest.

8. Before the soccer game, the players stretched.

9. Through the dense forest bends a narrow, rippling brook.

10. Were the children laughing at the silly cartoon?

Compound Verbs

1g. A ***compound verb*** consists of two or more verbs that are joined by a connecting word and that have the same subject.

A connecting word such as *and* or *but* joins the parts of a compound verb.

> **EXAMPLES** We **shouted** and **cheered** for our team. [*Shouted* and *cheered* both tell something about We.]
>
> Pete **had tossed** the basketball but **had missed** the basket. [*Had tossed* and *had missed* tell something about Pete.]

EXERCISE C Underline each part of the compound verb in the following sentences. Hint: Do not underline the connecting word that joins the parts of the verb.

Example 1. Mom was walking along the beach and talking with people. [*Was walking* and *talking* tell something about Mom.]

11. We enjoyed our family vacation and will remember it fondly. [Which words are the main words in the complete predicate?]

12. My older brother Carlos surfed the big waves or read a book.

13. I fished a few times but caught nothing.

14. In the evenings, we took walks, told stories, or sang songs.

15. Will your family go to the beach this summer or hike in the mountains?

    Introductory Course

The Noun

Nouns

2a. A ***noun*** is a word or word group that is used to name a person, place, thing, or idea.

PERSONS	brothers, Cindy, doctor, Ms. O'Connor
PLACES	park, San Diego Zoo, store, Mid-Cities Mall
THINGS	mailbox, Baltic Sea, mouse, Main Street
IDEAS	truth, humor, freedom, friendship

Did you notice that some of the nouns listed above are made up of more than one word? A *compound noun* is a single noun made up of two or more words. The compound noun may be written as one word, as a hyphenated word, or as two or more words.

ONE WORD	baseball, notebook, windsurfing
HYPHENATED WORD	self-respect, sister-in-law, runner-up
TWO WORDS	South America, middle school, boiler room

TIP To decide whether a word is a noun, try placing it in the blanks in the following sentences. If the word makes sense in at least one of the sentences, then the word is probably a noun.

EXAMPLES	I got a new _______. or I like _______.
	I got a new *backpack*. I like *loyalty*.

EXERCISE A Underline each noun in the following sentences. Remember to underline all parts of a compound noun. Hint: The title of a book is a noun.

Examples 1. <u>Alan</u> frequently reads <u>books</u> about <u>action</u> and <u>adventure</u>. [*Alan* names a person. *Books* names a thing. *Action* and *adventure* name ideas.]

2. <u>Alan</u> and his <u>friends</u> recently discovered the <u>author</u> <u>Will Hobbs</u>. [The nouns in this sentence name people.]

1. Will Hobbs has written many great books for young readers. [Which words name people and things?]

2. What excitement the children in the stories experience! [Which words name people, things, and ideas?]

3. In *Ghost Canoe*, Nathan MacAllister investigates a shipwreck.

4. Nathan and his mother live with the Makah Indians near the Pacific Ocean.

5. After a ship crashes on the rocks near the shore, strange events occur.

6. Who is the wild, hairy man that is hiding in the caves?

7. Captain Bim, a neighbor, buries treasures during the night.

8. A skeleton in an old canoe is discovered in a strange place: high in a tree.

9. Nathan and Lighthouse George search for clues to these mysteries.

10. Nathan shows great bravery and self-reliance during his adventure.

Common Nouns and Proper Nouns

You may have noticed that some nouns are capitalized and others are not. A ***common noun*** names any one of a group of persons, places, things, or ideas. A common noun is generally not capitalized. A ***proper noun*** names a particular person, place, thing, or idea. A proper noun begins with a capital letter. Proper nouns are often made up of more than one word.

   COMMON NOUNS   bridge, girl, holiday, continent, city

   PROPER NOUNS   Golden Gate Bridge, Anne Frank, Hanukkah, Africa, Salt Lake City

TIP▶ To identify a proper noun, try placing *a* or *an* in front of the noun. If *a* or *an* does not make sense in front of the noun, the noun is probably a proper noun. For example, *a San Francisco* doesn't make sense. Therefore, *San Francisco* is a proper noun.

EXERCISE B   Underline each common noun once in the following sentences. Underline each proper noun twice. Be sure to underline all parts of a compound noun.

Examples 1. Gloria Byrd and Marcus Katz spent the day at Rosemont Mall. [*Gloria Byrd* and *Marcus Katz* name specific people and are capitalized. *Day* names any one of a group of days and is not capitalized. *Rosemont Mall* names a specific place and is capitalized.]

     2. The two friends visited shops and looked at displays in the windows. [*Friends* names any of a group of people and is not capitalized. *Shops, displays,* and *windows* name any of a group of things and are not capitalized.]

11. Gloria and Christina Santos had first planned the trip to the mall. [Which nouns name specific people? Which nouns name any one of a group of places or things?]

12. At the last minute, Christina couldn't go. [Which noun names a specific person? Which noun names any one of a group of things?]

13. Gloria called Marcus, who lives nearby on Shepherd Lane.

14. Mrs. Byrd took both friends to the mall.

15. First, Gloria wanted to look at sneakers at Foot Market.

16. Next, she and Marcus browsed through the books, maps, and magazines at Skyline Bookstore.

17. Gloria found a fantastic book on the solar system.

18. Later, the two teenagers met Mrs. Byrd at the food court.

19. The book gave the girl self-confidence for her speech on the planets the next week.

20. The book was definitely cited in her report for Ms. Saunders.

8

Personal, Reflexive, and Intensive Pronouns

Personal Pronouns

2b.   A *pronoun* is a word that is used in place of one or more nouns or other pronouns.

> **EXAMPLE**   Chase said that **he** must study this weekend. [The pronoun *he* is used in place of the noun *Chase*.]

A *personal pronoun* refers to the one speaking (*first person*), the one spoken to (*second person*), or the one spoken about (*third person*).

> **FIRST PERSON**   **We** were sure that the birds would eat the bread. [The personal pronoun *We* refers to the people speaking.]
>
> **SECOND PERSON**   **Your** dad is on the phone. [The personal pronoun *Your* refers to the person to whom someone is speaking.]
>
> **THIRD PERSON**   Holly and Jon got to school early and talked with **their** friends. [The personal pronoun *their* refers to the people, *Holly and Jon*, about whom someone is speaking.]

EXERCISE A Underline the personal pronouns in each of the following sentences. Hint: Some sentences have more than one pronoun.

Examples   **1.** Do <u>you</u> know what a chapbook is? [The personal pronoun *you* refers to the person to whom someone is speaking.]

          2. <u>Our</u> teacher told <u>us</u> about chapbooks. [The personal pronouns *Our* and *us* refer to the people speaking.]

1. Chapbooks got their name from the chapmen who sold them. [Which words refer to a noun and are personal pronouns?]

2. Have you heard of chapmen? [Which word refers to the person to whom someone is speaking?]

3. They traveled around and sold chapbooks.

4. People bought inexpensive chapbooks for their own entertainment.

5. A chapbook was small; its pages measured approximately five inches by four inches.

6. A person could read about his or her favorite hero in a chapbook.

7. Ms. Williams told us about the jokes, rhymes, and stories in chapbooks.

8. The students said, "We will make our own chapbooks."

9. All students will collect their stories in a chapbook.

10. Lucinda and I asked to put pictures in our chapbooks.

GO ON ➤

Reflexive and Intensive Pronouns

A *reflexive pronoun* refers to the subject of a sentence. A reflexive pronoun is necessary to the basic meaning of the sentence. An *intensive pronoun* emphasizes the word to which it refers. An intensive pronoun is unnecessary to the basic meaning of the sentence.

REFLEXIVE PRONOUN   They recognized **themselves** in the photo. [The reflexive pronoun *themselves* refers to the subject, *They. Themselves* is necessary to the basic meaning of the sentence.]

INTENSIVE PRONOUN   She **herself** built the bookcase. [The intensive pronoun *herself* emphasizes *She. Herself* is not necessary to the basic meaning of the sentence.]

TIP▶ If you're not sure whether a pronoun is reflexive or intensive, use this test:

(1) Read the sentence aloud, leaving out the pronoun.
(2) If the meaning of the sentence stayed basically the same, the pronoun is intensive. If the meaning changed, the pronoun is reflexive.

EXAMPLES   We treated **ourselves** to lunch. [*Ourselves* refers to *We*. Without *ourselves*, the sentence doesn't make sense. The pronoun is reflexive.]

The boys washed the car **themselves.** [*Themselves* emphasizes *boys*. Without *themselves*, the meaning stays basically the same. The pronoun is intensive.]

EXERCISE B Identify the underlined pronoun in each of the following sentences. Write *REF* for *reflexive* or *INT* for *intensive* on the line provided.

Examples _*REF*_ **1.** Carla promised <u>herself</u> a fun weekend. [The pronoun *herself* refers to *Carla* and is necessary to the basic meaning of the sentence.]

*INT* **2.** The mayor <u>himself</u> made the announcement. [The pronoun *himself* emphasizes *mayor* and is not necessary to the basic meaning of the sentence.]

________ **11.** I saved the last apple for <u>myself</u>. [Without *myself*, does the meaning change?]

________ **12.** Kim had prepared the lunch <u>herself</u>. [Without *herself*, does the meaning change?]

________ **13.** We <u>ourselves</u> had not seen the exhibit at the museum.

________ **14.** That kite is flying all by <u>itself</u>!

________ **15.** Please help <u>yourself</u> to some juice.

________ **16.** Did Jimmy lock the door <u>himself</u> before leaving home?

________ **17.** I heard <u>myself</u> on the tape recorder for the first time.

________ **18.** You <u>yourselves</u> know what great actions you are capable of performing.

________ **19.** She often watches <u>herself</u> in the mirror as she dances.

________ **20.** The class arranged <u>themselves</u> in a large circle.

Demonstrative and Relative Pronouns

Demonstrative Pronouns

A *demonstrative pronoun* points out a specific person, place, thing, or idea. Demonstrative pronouns are *this, that, these,* and *those.*

EXAMPLES   Whose sweater is **this**? [*This* points out *sweater.*]

That is the new teacher. [*That* points out *teacher.*]

Those are the rules. [*Those* points out *rules.*]

Are **these** your gloves? [*These* points out *gloves.*]

TIP▶ To recognize a demonstrative pronoun, use this trick. If you could point at something while saying the pronoun, then the pronoun is probably demonstrative.

DEMONSTRATIVE   **That** is my favorite picture on the wall. [You might be pointing to a picture while saying the word *that. That* is a demonstrative pronoun.]

EXERCISE A   Underline the demonstrative pronoun in each of the following sentences.

Examples 1. Are <u>these</u> the sandwiches for our picnic? [The pronoun *these* points out *sandwiches.*]

2. <u>That</u> is the signal we will use in the game. [The pronoun *That* points out *signal.*]

1. That is the Gateway Arch in St. Louis, Missouri. [Which pronoun points out a thing?]

2. This is my new friend, Alex. [Which pronoun points out a person?]

3. What is that?

4. Are these the ingredients for your famous taco casserole?

5. Those are skid marks from someone's tires.

6. These are important qualities in a friend: loyalty and honesty.

7. Is that the sweater you are wearing with the new skirt?

8. This is the capital city of Wyoming.

9. These were found in the gym after the volleyball game.

10. Are those the buses for our field trip?

GO ON ➡

Relative Pronouns

A *relative pronoun* introduces an adjective clause. An adjective clause describes or adds information about the noun or pronoun that comes before it. Common relative pronouns include *that*, *which*, *who*, *whom*, and *whose*.

> **EXAMPLES**   Summer is the season **that** I like most. [The relative pronoun *that* introduces the adjective clause *that I like most*. The adjective clause adds information about the noun *season*.]
>
> Shawna Frost, **who** is our art teacher, is Matt's aunt. [The relative pronoun *who* introduces the adjective clause *who is our art teacher*. The adjective clause adds information about the woman *Shawna Frost*.]

EXERCISE B Identify each underlined pronoun in the following sentences. Write *DEM* on the line if the pronoun is demonstrative or *REL* if the pronoun is relative. Remember that the word *that* can be a demonstrative pronoun or a relative pronoun. Be careful to identify the word *that* correctly.

Examples *REL* **1.** The neighbors <u>whom</u> the Bensons met had moved here from Iowa. [The

relative pronoun *whom* introduces the adjective clause *whom the Bensons met*.]

DEM **2.** Are <u>those</u> the deer's footprints? [The demonstrative pronoun *those* points to

footprints.]

_______ **11.** The garden gate, <u>which</u> was not locked, banged in the wind. [Does the pronoun point to

something, or does it introduce an adjective clause?]

_______ **12.** <u>This</u> is a book about gold mines in the nineteenth century. [Does the pronoun point to

something, or does it introduce an adjective clause?]

_______ **13.** Nancy Tilden, <u>who</u> won the tennis match, is Gabriella's best friend.

_______ **14.** The man <u>whose</u> sofa Rob bought was moving to a smaller apartment.

_______ **15.** <u>That</u> is a poem by Lindsey Martin.

_______ **16.** The poem <u>that</u> Lindsey wrote is quite beautiful.

_______ **17.** <u>Those</u> are the winners of the photography contest.

_______ **18.** The friends <u>whom</u> Latonya invited to the party accepted the invitation.

_______ **19.** Are <u>these</u> the tips for today's grammar lesson?

_______ **20.** Is <u>that</u> Chen's scrapbook from the sixth grade?

Indefinite and Interrogative Pronouns

Indefinite Pronouns

Personal pronouns refer to specific people, places, things, or ideas. An ***indefinite pronoun*** refers to a person, place, thing, or idea that may or may not be specifically named.

> **EXAMPLES** **No one** had eaten lunch yet. [The indefinite pronoun *No one* does not refer to a specific person.]
>
> **Something** was different about the room. [The indefinite pronoun *Something* does not refer to a specific thing.]
>
> I do not know **anything** about the trip yet. [The indefinite pronoun *anything* does not refer to a specific thing.]

Common Indefinite Pronouns

all	each	more	one
any	either	much	other
anybody	everybody	neither	several
anyone	everyone	nobody	some
anything	few	none	somebody
both	many	no one	something

EXERCISE A Underline the indefinite pronoun in each of the following sentences.

Examples 1. Either of these nets will catch the insects. [The indefinite pronoun *Either* does not refer to a specific thing.]

2. The swift dragonfly could be caught by no one. [The indefinite pronoun *no one* does not refer to a specific person.]

1. Everybody had seen the beautiful dragonflies. [Which word is a pronoun and doesn't refer to a specific person?]

2. Several were flying by the pond. [Which word is a pronoun and doesn't refer to a specific thing?]

3. Bright colors marked the lower side of each of the dragonflies.

4. Somebody pointed out the two pairs of wings on the dragonflies.

5. Few knew that dragonflies lay eggs.

6. All of the eggs are laid on plants in fresh water, such as a pond.

7. None of the baby dragonflies, which are called nymphs, can fly yet.

8. The nymphs eat some of the other creatures in the pond.

9. None live in the pond for their whole life.

10. Each develops wings and flies away.

Interrogative Pronouns

An *interrogative pronoun* introduces a question.

EXAMPLES **What** is the name of this gemstone?

Who wrote *Night of the Twisters*?

To **whom** did you send the postcard?

Which of the CDs did you buy?

Whose is this phone number?

Interrogative Pronouns

what	which	who	whom	whose

EXERCISE B Identify each underlined pronoun in the following sentences. Write *INTER* if the pronoun is interrogative or *IND* if the pronoun is indefinite on the line provided.

Examples *INTER* **1.** For <u>whom</u> did you buy the gift? [The interrogative pronoun *whom* introduces a question.]

IND **2.** I don't know <u>anything</u> about that author. [The indefinite pronoun *anything* does not refer to a specific thing.]

_______ **11.** <u>Which</u> of these musical instruments can you play? [Does the pronoun introduce a question, or does it refer to something that is not specific?]

_______ **12.** <u>Many</u> of the students in my homeroom ride the same bus as I do. [Does the pronoun introduce a question, or does it refer to something that is not specific?]

_______ **13.** <u>Whose</u> is the umbrella beside the door?

_______ **14.** Do you want <u>either</u> of these magazines?

_______ **15.** <u>Who</u> volunteered for the fund-raiser?

_______ **16.** <u>Both</u> of my cousins go to my school.

_______ **17.** As she walked through the halls, she smiled at <u>everyone</u>.

_______ **18.** Late in summer, <u>much</u> of the lawn is dry and brown.

_______ **19.** About <u>whom</u> did Jerry write his essay?

_______ **20.** <u>Neither</u> wanted the last piece of chicken.

The Adjective

2c. An *adjective* is a word that is used to modify a noun or a pronoun.

To *modify* a word means to describe the word or to make its meaning more definite. An adjective modifies a noun or a pronoun by telling *what kind, which one, how many,* or *how much.*

WHAT KIND? **sunny** day, **blue** eyes, **British** writer, **kind** person

WHICH ONE OR ONES? **those** students, **second** one, **that** hat, **any** volunteer

HOW MANY? OR HOW MUCH? **some** pencils, **two** bears, **no** e-mails, **much** happiness

NOTE The words *a, an,* and *the* are adjectives.

EXERCISE A Underline each adjective in the following sentences. Do not underline *a, an,* or *the.* Some sentences may have more than one adjective.

Examples 1. Most students in the sixth grade have had a pet. [The adjective *Most* tells how many students. The adjective *sixth* tells which grade.]

2. A Korean student has a shy crab that is called a hermit. [The adjective *Korean* tells what kind of student. The adjective *shy* tells what kind of crab.]

1. Many people have a cat or a dog as a pet. [Which word describes a noun or pronoun?]

2. Cody, however, has a white rabbit as a pet. [Which word describes a noun or pronoun?]

3. The small rabbit lives in a large pen in the bedroom.

4. A tiny doghouse serves as a cozy burrow for the rabbit.

5. Cody gives Thumper clean water every day.

6. Thumper eats fresh vegetables and special food for rabbits.

7. On quiet afternoons, Cody lets Thumper out of the pen.

8. Cody likes to pet the silky, soft fur that Thumper has.

9. During the short playtimes, Cody keeps Thumper away from dangerous places.

10. Thumper seems to enjoy the extra attention.

Adjectives usually come before the words they describe or modify. Sometimes, however, an adjective comes after the word it describes.

EXAMPLES These grapes are **sour.** [The adjective *sour* describes the noun *grapes.*]

The rug, **bright** and **colorful,** added cheer to the room. [The adjectives *bright* and *colorful* describe the noun *rug.*]

GO ON

EXERCISE B Underline each adjective in the following sentences. Then, draw an arrow from the adjective to the word or words it describes. Do not underline *a, an,* or *the.*

Examples 1. The river, icy and swift, lay before the two hikers. [The adjectives *icy* and *swift* describe *river.* The adjective *two* tells how many hikers.]

2. The wooden bridge was old and shaky. [The adjectives *wooden, old,* and *shaky* describe *bridge.*]

11. An empty cabin sat in a small meadow. [Which words describe a noun or pronoun?]

12. Nearby, the rapid river rushed between muddy banks. [Which words describe a noun or pronoun?]

13. The hikers, hungry and weary, stopped in the meadow.

14. They looked at the ancient bridge and deep water.

15. They wondered how they had gotten to the remote, lonely place.

16. The correct path through the woods wasn't clear.

17. One hiker, smart and practical, built a warm fire.

18. The other person unfolded a large map of the area.

19. One of them pulled a small compass and extra food from a backpack.

20. They ate food and drank fresh water, and they plotted a clear course home.

EXERCISE C Underline all of the adjectives in the following paragraph. Do not underline *a, an,* or *the.* One sentence has more than one adjective.

Example **[1]** In the gymnasium, the excited crowd cheered. [The word *excited* tells what kind of crowd.]

[In the paragraph's first sentence, which word tells what kind of sneakers?]

[21] As Juanita dribbled the basketball, her new sneakers squeaked. **[22]** She pretended to step one way, then changed directions at the last second. **[23]** An unlucky opponent tried to stop Juanita, but could not. **[24]** Juanita shot the ball and made an easy basket. **[25]** The smooth ball barely touched the net as it flew through the air.

for CHAPTER 3: PARTS OF SPEECH OVERVIEW `pages 95–96`

The Verb

What Is a Verb?

3a. A *verb* is a word that expresses action or a state of being.

EXAMPLES We **played** a game of basketball. [The verb *played* expresses the action we performed.]

Throughout the game, my team **was** awesome! [The verb *was* does not express an action. Instead, it expresses something about the team's state of being.]

EXERCISE A Underline the verb in each of the following sentences.

Examples 1. Lydia was at her uncle's farm. [The verb *was* expresses something about Lydia's state of being.]

2. She saw a wonderful red barn near the farmhouse. [The verb *saw* expresses the action she performed.]

1. Lydia and her cousin walked over to the barn one evening. [Which word expresses the action Lydia and her cousin performed?]

2. Several stalls were on one side of the barn. [Which word expresses something about the stalls' state of being?]

3. Lydia looked into the first stall.

4. A large brown horse stood inside.

5. Its name was Starfire.

6. Starfire belonged to Lydia's uncle.

7. Lydia and her cousin put fresh hay in Starfire's stall every morning.

8. Sometimes, Lydia's cousin brings out her horse, Thunder.

9. Thunder is a very gentle horse.

10. Lydia and her cousin give Thunder a lot of attention.

Helping Verbs and Main Verbs

The main verb is the word that expresses action or state of being. Sometimes, other verbs are added to the main verb to make the main verb more specific. These other verbs are called helping verbs. A *helping verb* helps the main verb express action or state of being.

NOTE *Helping verbs are sometimes called auxiliary verbs.*

GO ON

Commonly Used Helping Verbs

am	being	do	have	must	were
are	can	does	is	shall	will
be	could	had	may	should	would
been	did	has	might	was	

> **EXAMPLES**   Helen **will** attend the music recital. [The helping verb *will* helps the main verb *attend* express a future action.]
>
> Pedro **should** be here soon. [The helping verb *should* helps the main verb *be* express an expected state of being.]

A *verb phrase* contains at least one main verb and one or more helping verbs.

> **EXAMPLES**   The car **was driving** uphill. [*Was driving* is the verb phrase. The helping verb is *was*, and the main verb is *driving*.]
>
> **Did** you **finish** your homework? [*Did finish* is the verb phrase. The helping verb is *Did*, and the main verb is *finish*.]
>
> Shoes **must be worn** inside the cafe. [*Must be worn* is the verb phrase. The helping verbs are *must* and *be*, and the main verb is *worn*.]

EXERCISE B Underline the verb phrase in each of the following sentences. Then, draw a second line under the helping verb or verbs.

Examples 1. When <u>will</u> we <u>be writing</u> a report on our home state? [The verb phrase is *will be writing*. The helping verbs are *will* and *be*, and the main verb is *writing*.]

2. You <u>can look</u> for information in the library and on the Internet. [The verb phrase is *can look*. The helping verb is *can*, and the main verb is *look*.]

11. What information could Toby find about Nebraska? [Which word expresses the action? What other verb is helping it?]

12. He had been studying an atlas. [Which word expresses the action? What other verbs are helping it?]

13. Do you know the history of Nebraska's name?

14. The Oto Indians had named one of the rivers *Nebrathka*.

15. Today, this river is known as the Platte River.

16. We have taken the name for Nebraska from *Nebrathka*.

17. Toby was finding other facts.

18. For instance, Buffalo Bill had made his home in Nebraska.

19. A large mammoth fossil had been found in the southwestern area of the state.

20. Arbor Day was begun by a Nebraskan, Julius Sterling Morton.

Action Verbs and Linking Verbs

Action Verbs

Verbs can be identified as action verbs or linking verbs.

An *action verb* expresses either physical or mental activity.

> **EXAMPLES** Dad **made** oat bran muffins for breakfast. [The verb *made* shows physical action.]
>
> Teresa **daydreams** of adventure. [The verb *daydreams* shows mental action.]

REMINDER When you identify action verbs, remember to include any helping verbs. Helping verbs are added to the main verb to make the main verb more specific.

> **EXAMPLES** **Did** you **understand** the short story's ending? [The main verb is *understand,* and the helping verb is *Did.* The verb phrase *Did understand* shows mental action.]
>
> Mom **is mowing** the lawn. [The main verb is *mowing,* and the helping verb is *is.* The verb phrase *is mowing* shows physical action.]

EXERCISE A Underline the action verbs in each of the following sentences. Remember to include any helping verbs.

Examples 1. Are the players jogging around the track? [The verb phrase *Are jogging* expresses the action the players perform.]

2. During December, Marty constantly thinks about skiing. [The verb *thinks* expresses the action Marty performs.]

1. Thorns grow on the stem of a rose. [Which word expresses the action the thorns perform?]

2. Did the newspaper staff meet their deadline? [Which words express the action the staff performs?]

3. We named our new puppy Peanuts.

4. The flowers are blooming now.

5. Did you volunteer at the food bank?

6. The history students have not presented their reports yet.

7. On winter evenings, the farmer feeds hay to his cows.

8. Ms. Kaufmann's secretary has a message for her.

9. We have formed a plan for the autumn carnival.

10. On the bus, we usually talk about friends and activities.

GO ON

Linking Verbs

A *linking verb* connects, or links, the subject to a word or word group that identifies or describes the subject.

Some Linking Verbs Formed from the Verb *Be*

am	was	have been	shall be	can be
is	were	had been	may be	should be
are	has been	will be	might be	would have been

Other Linking Verbs

appear	grow	seem	stay
become	look	smell	taste
feel	remain	sound	turn

> **EXAMPLES** My favorite musical **is** *My Fair Lady*. [The linking verb *is* connects the subject, *musical*, to the word group, *My Fair Lady*, that identifies it.]
>
> Dinner **had tasted** delicious. [The linking verb *had tasted* connects the subject, *dinner*, to the word, *delicious*, that describes it.]

EXERCISE B Underline the linking verbs in the following sentences. Remember to include any helping verbs. Hint: Helping verbs are verbs that are added to the main verb to make the main verb more specific.

Examples 1. <u>Was</u> Carla the winner? [The linking verb *Was* connects the subject, *Carla*, to the word, *winner*, that identifies her.]

2. He <u>had seemed</u> happy with his grade. [The main verb is *seemed*, and the helping verb is *had*. The linking verb *had seemed* links the subject, *He*, to the word, *happy*, that describes him.]

11. Lee will be Aunt Juanita's assistant this summer. [Which words link *Lee* to *assistant*?]

12. Aunt Juanita is a landscape architect. [Which words link *Aunt Juanita* to *architect*?]

13. Photographs of her designs are special features in many landscaping magazines.

14. Her business has become a great success.

15. She was extremely busy last year.

16. Her designs look unique.

17. Has anyone ever been unhappy with her work?

18. Her backyard is a work of art.

19. Does the flowing water sound peaceful to you?

20. The flowers and herbs smell wonderful.

20

The Adverb

What Is an Adverb?

| **3b.** | An **adverb** is a word that modifies a verb, an adjective, or another adverb. |

REMINDER ▶ A *verb* is a word or word group that expresses action or state of being. An *adjective* is a word that modifies or describes a noun or pronoun.

To *modify* a word means to describe it or make its meaning more specific. Adverbs make the meaning of a verb, adjective, or another adverb more definite. Adverbs answer the following questions: Where? How often? How long? When? To what extent? How much? How?

EXAMPLES   Cindy strolled along the shore, and she **frequently** stopped to collect shells.

[The adverb *frequently* modifies the verb *stopped* and tells *how often*.]

Was the auditorium **completely** full **yesterday**? [The adverb *completely*

modifies the adjective *full* and tells *how much*. The adverb *yesterday*

modifies the verb *was* and tells *when*.]

EXERCISE A   Underline the adverbs in the following sentences.

Examples 1. Some people make friends quickly. [The adverb *quickly* modifies the verb *make* and

tells *how long*.]

2. However, I am quite shy. [The adverb *quite* modifies the adjective *shy* and tells *to what*

extent.]

1. My family recently moved to a new town. [Which word tells when my family moved?]

2. I have been carefully exploring my new neighborhood. [Which word tells how I have been

exploring?]

3. The Moore twins have been very friendly.

4. How often have they invited me to play sports with them?

5. They are quite fond of softball.

6. Sometimes, I go to the local library.

7. What a wonderful selection of books they have there!

8. The librarian is really helpful.

9. I could probably join the club for teen readers.

10. I have already read many of the books on the list.

GO ON ➡

Position of Adverbs

Adverbs may come before, after, or between the words they modify.

EXAMPLES   **Quietly,** the cat was stalking a bird. [*Quietly* comes before *was stalking*, the verb phrase it modifies.]

The cat was stalking a bird **quietly.** [*Quietly* comes after *was stalking*, the verb phrase it modifies.]

The cat was **quietly** stalking a bird. [*Quietly* comes between *was* and *stalking*, the verb phrase it modifies.]

TIP Many adverbs end in –*ly*. When you come across a word that ends in –*ly*, check to see if this word describes another word. If the –*ly* word describes a verb, an adjective, or another adverb, then the –*ly* word is an adverb.

EXERCISE B Draw an arrow from the underlined adverb in each of the following sentences to the word or words it modifies. Hint: An adverb modifies each word in a verb phrase, not just the main verb. If the adverb modifies a verb phrase, be sure to draw an arrow from the adverb to each part of the verb.

Examples 1. I did <u>not</u> forget what happened. [The adverb *not* modifies the verb *did forget* and tells *to what extent*.]

2. <u>Frequently</u>, my neighbors have a garage sale. [The adverb *frequently* modifies the verb *have* and tells *how often*.]

11. My family <u>seldom</u> travels out of state. [*Seldom* tells *how often* about which word?]

12. Did all the balloons float <u>away</u>? [*Away* tells *where* about which words?]

13. The gymnast can <u>easily</u> perform his routines.

14. Richard was <u>slowly</u> pronouncing the words in German.

15. My brother is <u>rarely</u> sick.

16. Will your sister attend college <u>soon</u>?

17. He has memorized <u>nearly</u> all his lines for the school play.

18. I <u>hardly</u> recognized my cousin at the family reunion.

19. That movie was <u>really</u> funny!

20. We had <u>not</u> read *The View from Saturday*.

The Preposition

Prepositions

3c. | A *preposition* is a word that shows the relationship between a noun or a pronoun and another word in the sentence.

> **EXAMPLES** The pilot climbed **into** the cockpit. [The preposition *into* shows the relationship between *climbed* and *cockpit*.]
>
> Here is a letter **from** Julie. [The preposition *from* shows the relationship between *letter* and *Julie*.]

By using different prepositions, you can change the relationship between *walked* and *puddle* in the following sentences.

Alex walked **around** the puddle.   Alex walked **toward** the puddle.
Alex walked **through** the puddle.   Alex walked **past** the puddle.

Commonly Used Prepositions

above	before	down	of	under
across	behind	for	on	underneath
after	below	from	since	until
against	beside	in	through	up
around	between	into	throughout	with
at	by	like	to	without

EXERCISE A Underline the prepositions in each of the following sentences. Hint: Some sentences have more than one preposition.

Examples 1. Some people feel nervous <u>around</u> computers. [The preposition *around* shows the relationship between *nervous* and *computers*.]

2. They may need help <u>with</u> the commands or a lesson <u>on</u> the software. [The preposition *with* shows the relationship between *help* and *commands*. The preposition *on* shows the relationship between *lesson* and *software*.]

1. Rosa seated herself by her grandmother's computer. [Which word shows the relationship between *herself* and *computer*?]

2. Several items were stacked beside the monitor. [Which word shows the relationship between *stacked* and *monitor*?]

3. "Where is the program you want installed on your computer?" Rosa asked her grandmother.

4. Her grandmother handed her a CD inside a plastic case.

5. Rosa placed the CD into the CD-ROM drive on the computer.

6. After a few seconds, a dialog box appeared on the screen.

Developmental Language Skills

7. She followed the prompts on the monitor.

8. Behind her chair stood her grandmother.

9. Finally, Rosa relaxed against the chair's back.

10. "Grandma, your new computer program is ready for you."

Compound Prepositions

Some prepositions are made up of more than one word. These are called *compound prepositions.*

    EXAMPLES   A rose bush grew **next to** the fence. [The preposition *next to* shows the
             relationship of *grew* to *fence.*]

             The story **according to** Janice is different. [The preposition *according to*
             shows the relationship of *story* to *Janice.*]

Some Compound Prepositions

according to	because of	in place of	next to	out of
aside from	in addition to	in spite of	on account of	

EXERCISE B Underline the preposition(s) in each of the following sentences. Remember to underline all words in a compound preposition.

Examples 1. The closet beneath the stairs is tiny. [The preposition *beneath* shows the relationship

         between *closet* and *stairs.*]

    2. I enjoyed the book in spite of its length. [The compound preposition *in spite of* shows

         the relationship between *enjoyed* and *length.*]

11. Aside from one problem, the event went smoothly. [Which words show the relationship between

     smoothly and *problem*?]

12. I found the remote control underneath the sofa. [Which word shows the relationship between

     found and *sofa*?]

13. How many books have fallen out of my backpack?

14. Sometimes, I eat tofu in place of meat.

15. How beautiful those flowers look next to the gray walls!

16. Is the bridge closed due to the flood?

17. The building next to my school is empty.

18. There are cabins throughout the campground.

19. In addition to a pillow and clothes, you'll need a sleeping bag.

20. The guy with the big smile is my best friend.

The Conjunction and the Interjection

Coordinating Conjunctions

3d. A *conjunction* is a word that joins words or groups of words.

> **EXAMPLES**   Ask the librarian **or** your teacher for information about the essay contest.
>
> Leah volunteers at the animal shelter, **and** she often adopts animals.

A *coordinating conjunction* joins words or word groups that are used in the same way. Coordinating conjunctions join words to words, phrases to phrases, and clauses to clauses.

Some common coordinating conjunctions are *and, but, for, nor, or, so,* and *yet.*

> **EXAMPLES**   shy **but** friendly [The conjunction *but* joins two words.]
>
> doing homework **and** listening to music [The conjunction *and* joins two phrases.]
>
> I arrived early, **so** I waited patiently. [The conjunction *so* joins two clauses.]

EXERCISE A   Underline the coordinating conjunction in each of the following sentences.

Example 1. The children were restless, for they had been indoors several hours. [The conjunction *for* joins two clauses.]

1. Diego prepared a meal of chicken and rice. [Which word joins *chicken* and *rice*?]

2. Ellen was tired, yet she ran one more lap around the track.

3. The car gets good gas mileage and is reasonably priced.

4. The afternoon was beautiful, so I went for a walk.

5. The survivors of the shipwreck didn't panic, nor did they give up hope.

Correlative conjunctions

Correlative conjunctions are pairs of conjunctions. The pairs work together to join words or word groups that are used in the same way. They join words to words, phrases to phrases, and clauses to clauses.

Correlative Conjunctions

both… and	either… or	neither… nor
not only… but also	whether… or	

> **EXAMPLES**   **Both** the *Pioneer* **and** the *Hunley* were submarines in the Civil War. [The correlative conjunctions *both . . . and* join two words.]
>
> Suzette is saving money **not only** for a pet **but also** for pet supplies. [The correlative conjunctions *not only . . . but also* join two phrases.]
>
> **Either** the house is haunted **or** there is a more scientific explanation. [The correlative conjunctions *Either . . . or* join two clauses.]

GO ON

EXERCISE B Underline the correlative conjunctions in each of the following sentences. Remember to underline both parts of correlative conjunctions.

Example 1. The band will perform whether it's beautiful outside or it's raining. [The correlative

conjunctions *whether…or* join two clauses.]

6. Not only could the contestant dance, but he could also sing. [Which words join the clauses *the

contestant could dance* and *he could sing*?]

7. Either the kayak or the canoe will be perfect for an outing on the lake.

8. Both George Bush and his son George W. Bush have been elected President.

9. I can't tell whether this is lemon or this is lime.

10. Neither Raul nor Sue has any brothers or sisters.

Interjections

3e. An *interjection* is a word that expresses emotion.

An interjection can be left out of a sentence without changing the meaning of the sentence. Commonly used interjections include *aha, ouch, wow, oh, yikes, hurray, oops, well,* and *yippee.*

Interjections that express strong emotions are followed by an exclamation point.

> **EXAMPLES Wow!** What an exciting game that was!
> I stepped in mud. **Yuck!**
> **Hey!** What are you doing?

Interjections that express mild emotion are set off from the rest of a sentence by commas.

> **EXAMPLES Well,** I will try my best.
> I have, **oh,** about five dollars.
> Our adventure is over, **alas.**

EXERCISE C Underline the interjection in each of the following sentences.

Example 1. Yikes! That hill seems a mile high. [The interjection *Yikes* expresses a strong emotion.]

11. Hurray! Our team placed first at the competition. [Which word expresses a strong emotion?]

12. This water is cold and, oh, feels great on my tired feet.

13. Aw, those kittens are so cute!

14. I almost missed the bus. Whew!

15. Goodness! You startled me.

The Prepositional Phrase

Phrases

4a. A *phrase* is a group of related words that is used as a single part of speech and that does not contain both a verb and its subject.

> **PHRASES** had been whispering [no subject]
>
> in my closet [no subject or verb]
>
> beside the CD player [no subject or verb]

Phrases cannot stand alone as sentences. They must be used with other words to make a complete sentence.

> **PHRASE** throughout the countryside [The phrase cannot stand alone as a sentence.]
>
> **SENTENCE** The good news spread **throughout the countryside.** [The phrase is used with other words to make a complete sentence.]

NOTE▶ If a word group has both a subject and its verb, it is not a phrase. Such a word group is called a *clause.*

> **CLAUSES** Samuel hurried home. [*Samuel* is the subject of the verb *hurried.*]
>
> After Isabel left school that day [*Isabel* is the subject of the verb *left.*]

EXERCISE A Identify each of the following word groups as a phrase or not a phrase. Write *P* for *phrase* or *NP* for *not a phrase* on the lines provided.

Examples ___*P*___ **1.** of my favorite creatures [The word group does not contain a verb and its subject. The word group is a phrase.]

___*NP*___ **2.** that I recently learned [The word group contains a verb, *learned,* and its subject, *I.* Therefore, the word group is not a phrase.]

_______ **1.** was covering [Does the word group contain a verb and its subject?]

_______ **2.** from the north [Does the word group contain a verb and its subject?]

_______ **3.** before classes start today

_______ **4.** behind the door

_______ **5.** he opened the window

_______ **6.** has been walking

_______ **7.** because of its size

_______ **8.** that they can see

_______ **9.** to look at the exhibit

_______ **10.** with fruit and vegetables

GO ON ▶

Prepositional Phrases

4b.   A *prepositional phrase* includes a preposition, the object of the preposition, and any modifiers of that object.

A *preposition* is a word that shows the relationship of a noun or pronoun to another word in the sentence. The *object of the preposition* is the noun or pronoun that completes the prepositional phrase.

> **EXAMPLES**   A package **from Grandma** arrived today. [The preposition is *from*. The object is *Grandma*. The object is not modified by any words. The preposition and the object make up the prepositional phrase.]
>
> **On the counter and the floor** there was flour and rice. [The preposition is *on*. There are two objects, *counter* and *floor*. Both objects are modified by *the*. Together, these words make up the prepositional phrase.]

Common Prepositions

about	between	in	to
according to	by	in addition to	under
after	during	near	until
at	for	of	with
before	from	through	without

EXERCISE B   Underline the prepositional phrase in each of the following sentences.

Examples 1. There are a lot of coconut palm trees around the world. [One preposition is *of*. Its object is *coconut palm trees*. Another preposition is *around*. Its object is *world*.]

2. The coconut palm tree can grow to 100 feet. [The preposition is *to*. The object of the preposition is *feet*.]

11. Its trunk leans toward one side or the other. [Which word is a preposition? What are the objects of the preposition?]

12. This tree is usually found near sandy beaches. [Which word is a preposition? What is its object?]

13. In addition to green palm leaves, the tree produces coconuts.

14. Have you ever bought a whole coconut from a store or market?

15. Inside the husk and shell is the nut itself.

16. The nut resembles a white ball with a hollow center.

17. Within the center, the nut holds coconut milk.

18. Some people use the milk in special recipes.

19. Others drain the milk into the sink and then eat the nut.

20. I enjoy fresh, sweet coconut as a snack.

The Adjective Phrase

A phrase is a word group that does not contain both a verb and its subject.

4c. A prepositional phrase that modifies (or describes) a noun or pronoun is called an ***adjective phrase.***

An adjective phrase is a prepositional phrase that is used as an adjective.

ADJECTIVE	**Gold** coins filled the chest. [The adjective *Gold* describes the noun *coins*.]
ADJECTIVE PHRASE	Coins **of gold** filled the chest. [The adjective phrase *of gold* describes the noun *Coins*.]

An adjective phrase generally comes after the word it describes. An adjective phrase also answers the same questions that an adjective answers: *What kind? Which one? How many?* or *How much?*

EXAMPLES Did Kyle buy a CD **of classical music**? [The adjective phrase *of classical music* describes the noun *CD*. The phrase tells *what kind* of CD.]

A tray **of steamed vegetables** sat nearby. [The adjective phrase *of steamed vegetables* describes the noun *tray*. The phrase tells *what kind* of tray.]

EXERCISE A Draw an arrow from the underlined adjective phrase to the word it describes in each of the following sentences.

Examples 1. The woman in the red uniform took our tickets. [The adjective phrase *in the red uniform* describes the noun *woman*.]

2. Do you see the clowns in pink and yellow wigs? [The adjective phrase *in pink and yellow wigs* describes the noun *clowns*.]

1. The food from the vendor was delicious. [Which word does the adjective phrase describe?]

2. We entered the tent with the big top. [Which word does the adjective phrase describe?]

3. Are some of the front seats still available?

4. The trapeze artists near the ladder are extremely talented!

5. Watch the man on the unicycle.

6. A group of teenage performers entered the center ring.

7. Is the one in the black outfit their team captain?

8. A large crowd of people were watching a juggler.

9. The hall of mirrors looks fun.

10. Try the game with the silver rings.

More than one adjective phrase may describe the same noun or pronoun.

> **EXAMPLE**   Derek's speech **about outer space in science class** was excellent. [The two
> adjective phrases are *about outer space* and *in science class*. Each phrase
> describes the noun *speech* and tells *which* speech.]

An adjective phrase may describe the object of another adjective phrase.

> **EXAMPLE**   A book **from the top of the shelf** caught my attention. [The first adjective
> phrase is *from the top*. This phrase describes the noun *book* and tells *which*
> book. The second adjective phrase is *of the shelf*. This phrase describes
> the noun *top* and tells *which* top.]

EXERCISE B   Underline each adjective phrase in the following sentences. Then, draw an arrow from the
phrase to the word it describes. Some sentences have more than one adjective phrase.

Examples 1. *Alien Secrets* is a book about a teenager by Annette Curtis Klause. [The adjective
phrases *about a teenager* and *by Annette Curtis Klause* describe the noun *book*.]

2. Isn't this story about an adventure in outer space? [The adjective phrase *about an
adventure* describes the noun *story*. The adjective phrase *in outer space* describes the
noun *adventure*.]

11. The name of the main character is Puck. [Which word group is an adjective phrase? Which word
does it describe?]

12. The story recounts Puck's trip to another part of the universe. [Which two word groups are
adjective phrases? Which words do they describe?]

13. When she leaves school, the adventures of Puck truly begin.

14. Puck's parents are studying life on another planet.

15. Her best friend on the ship is Hush, an alien.

16. Together, they must solve the theft of a valuable piece of art.

17. Some police on the ship are working undercover.

18. Don't a number of alien ghosts haunt the ship?

19. Puck is the hero of this memorable story.

20. She displays the wisdom of a much older person.

The Adverb Phrase

A phrase is a word group that does not contain both a verb and its subject.

4d.   A prepositional phrase that is used to modify (or describe) a verb, an adjective, or an adverb is called an ***adverb phrase.***

An adverb phrase is a prepositional phrase that is used as an adverb.

> **ADVERB**   The police chief works **here.** [The adverb *here* describes the verb *works.*]
>
> **ADVERB PHRASE**   The police chief works **at his desk.** [The adverb phrase *at his desk* describes the verb *works.*]

Adverb phrases may come before or after the words they describe. Also, other words may come between an adverb phrase and the word it describes. An adverb phrase answers the same questions that an adverb answers: *When? Where? Why? How? How often?* and *How long?*

> **EXAMPLES**   Has the florist arrived **at his shop?** [The adverb phrase describes the verb *Has arrived* and answers the question *Where?*]
>
> Her sketches are famous **for their detail.** [The adverb phrase describes the adjective *famous* and answers the question *Why?*]
>
> That music is playing too loudly **for my preference.** [The adverb phrase describes the adverb *loudly* and answers the question *How?*]
>
> **During the eclipse,** the sky grew dark. [The adverb phrase describes the verb *grew* and answers the question *When?*]

EXERCISE A   Draw an arrow from the underlined adverb phrase to the word or words it describes.

Examples 1. Around the coral reef swam the fish. [The adverb phrase describes the verb *swam.*]

      2. Did Raul talk about the students' projects? [The adverb phrase describes the verb *Did talk.*]

1. The fans clapped with enthusiasm. [Which word does the adverb phrase describe?]

2. Cedric dropped a penny into the fountain. [Which word does the adverb phrase describe?]

3. This box is full of old clothes.

4. After the concert we ate frozen yogurt.

5. Wow! Jack caught the fly ball with one hand.

6. Decorate the bulletin board with paper snowflakes.

7. Nina was early for her dentist appointment.

8. High in the mountains is a beautiful waterfall.

GO ON

9. Had everyone arrived <u>before Keith</u>?

10. <u>Around my ears</u> buzzed a hungry mosquito.

More than one adverb phrase can describe the same word.

> **EXAMPLE**   We went **to lunch with Chi.** [Both adverb phrases, *to lunch* and *with Chi*,
>
> describe the verb *went*.]

Sometimes an adverb phrase is followed by an adjective phrase. The adjective phrase describes the object of the preposition in the adverb phrase.

> **EXAMPLE**   We ordered our meals **from the server with a red necktie.** [The adverb
> phrase *from the server* describes the verb *ordered* and tells *where*. The
> adjective phrase *with a red necktie* modifies the noun *server* and tells
> *which one.*]

EXERCISE B   Underline each adverb phrase in the following sentences. Then, draw an arrow from the phrase to the word it describes. Some sentences contain more than one adverb phrase. Remember that an adverb phrase describes a verb, an adjective, or an adverb.

Examples 1. Beneath the tree in the shade sat the friends. [Both adverb phrases describe the verb *sat*.]

2. Did they think of ideas for a group activity? [The adverb phrase modifies the verb

Did think.]

11. During the summer the heat grew fierce. [Which word group is an adverb phrase? Which word

does it describe?]

12. Then, Carlos told us about the new ice rink. [Which word group is an adverb phrase? Which

word does it describe?]

13. Has the ice rink opened to the public?

14. During the afternoon we went to the ice rink.

15. Rent your ice skates at the front desk.

16. As a child, I had skated on ice a few times.

17. At the rink we enjoyed ourselves on the ice.

18. My brother Raul has always been good at skating.

19. Did you bring gloves with you to the rink?

20. Follow me across the ice.

for **CHAPTER 4: THE PHRASE AND THE CLAUSE**   `pages 135–136`

The Clause

Independent Clauses

4e.   A *clause* is a word group that contains a verb and its subject and that is used as a sentence or as a part of a sentence.

Every clause contains a subject and a verb. However, not all clauses express complete thoughts. Clauses that express complete thoughts are called *independent clauses.* Clauses that do not express complete thoughts are called *subordinate clauses.*

4f.   An *independent* (or *main*) *clause* expresses a complete thought and can stand by itself as a sentence.

> **EXAMPLES**   **Rodney tells** funny jokes. [The subject is *Rodney,* and the verb is *tells.* The word group *Rodney tells funny jokes* expresses a complete thought and is, therefore, an independent clause.]
>
>   **He has entertained** us during lunch. [The subject is *He,* and the verb is *has entertained.* The word group *He has entertained us during lunch* expresses a complete thought and is, therefore, an independent clause.]

When an independent clause stands alone, it is called a sentence. Usually, the term *independent clause* is used only when such a clause is joined with another clause.

> **SENTENCE**   **She practices the flute.**
>
> **INDEPENDENT CLAUSE**   Before she eats dinner, **she practices the flute.** [The independent clause is *she practices the flute.* The entire word group is a sentence.]

EXERCISE A Decide whether each of the following word groups is an independent clause or is not an independent clause. Write *IND* for *independent clause* or *Not* for *not an independent clause* on the line provided.

Example   *IND* **1.** what did you eat for lunch [The word group has a subject, *you,* and a verb, *did eat.* It expresses a complete thought and can stand alone. Therefore, it is an independent clause.]

________ **1.** Sammy solved the problem [Does the word group have a verb and its subject? Does the word group express a complete thought, and can it stand alone?]

________ **2.** whether the shoe fits [Does the word group have a verb and its subject? Does the word group express a complete thought, and can it stand alone?]

________ **3.** with whom she sang at the concert

________ **4.** she chose a new hat

________ **5.** since Chris got a bicycle

________ **6.** my foot hurts

________ **7.** the book fair is tomorrow

                                                                GO ON ➡

_______ **8.** wherever you see the ants

_______ **9.** than Gracie did

_______ **10.** call me tonight after dinner

Subordinate Clauses

4g. A *subordinate* (or *dependent*) *clause* does not express a complete thought and cannot stand by itself as a complete sentence.

A subordinate clause has a verb and its subject, but the clause does not express a complete thought.

> **EXAMPLES** to whom I wrote [The subordinate clause has a verb, *wrote*, and its subject, *I*. However, the clause does not express a complete thought.]
>
> If you use the Internet [The subordinate clause has a verb, *use*, and its subject, *you*. However, the clause does not express a complete thought.]

A subordinate clause must be joined with at least one independent clause to make a sentence and express a complete thought.

> **EXAMPLES** Rosa is the friend **to whom I wrote.** [The subordinate clause *to whom I wrote* is joined with the independent clause *Rosa is the friend*. Together, they make a sentence.]
>
> **If you have time,** will you send me an e-mail? [The subordinate clause *If you use the Internet* is joined with the independent clause *will you send me an e-mail*. Together, they make a sentence.]

Common Words that Begin Subordinate Clauses

after	before	so that	when
as	how	than	who
because	if	that	while

EXERCISE B Identify each underlined word group as either an independent clause or a subordinate clause. Write *IND* for *independent clause* or *SUB* for *subordinate clause* on the line provided.

Example _IND_ **1.** The *Active* was the first train that carried passengers. [The underlined word group has a verb, *was*, and its subject, *Active*. It also expresses a complete thought and can stand alone. Therefore, it is an independent clause.]

_______ **11.** While we were on the highway, did you see the freight train? [Does the underlined word group express a complete thought, and can it stand alone?]

_______ **12.** Count the locomotives on a freight train as it passes in front of you.

_______ **13.** Have you heard of the longest freight train that has ever operated?

_______ **14.** You certainly were not born yet when this train was in use.

_______ **15.** It was nearly four miles long, and it ran in 1967.

The Adjective Clause

4h.   An *adjective clause* is a subordinate clause that modifies (or describes) a noun or pronoun.

Remember that a subordinate clause does not express a complete thought and cannot stand alone. An adjective clause works just like an adjective or an adjective phrase.

ADJECTIVE   I like **French** music. [The adjective *French* describes the noun *music*.]

ADJECTIVE PHRASE   I like music **from France.** [The adjective phrase *from France* describes the noun *music. From France* does not have a subject and verb.]

ADJECTIVE CLAUSE   I like music **that is from France.** [The adjective clause *that is from France* describes the noun *music*. The clause has a verb, *is*, and its subject, *that*.]

An adjective clause usually follows the noun or pronoun it describes. The clause tells *Which one?* or *What kind?*

EXAMPLES   These potatoes, **which have been boiled,** are for the potato salad. [The adjective clause describes the noun *potatoes* and tells *what kind*.]

I cleaned each one **that was dirty.** [The adjective clause describes the pronoun *one* and tells *which one*.]

EXERCISE A Draw an arrow from each underlined adjective clause to the noun or pronoun it describes.

Examples **1.** Luisa and I are "BFF," which means "best friends forever." [The adjective clause describes *"BFF."*]

  2. Why didn't they paint the side that faces north? [The adjective clause describes *side.*]

1. The last entertainer that performed was named Suzi. [Which word does the adjective clause describe?]

2. Look up the word in the dictionary, which is on the desk. [Which word does the adjective clause describe?]

3. Jim quickly wrote out the math problems that the teacher had assigned.

4. Have you learned some skills that help you on tests?

5. Is Marian one of the students whose grades have improved?

6. The students who sit in the front row will be team captains.

7. Let's listen to Rosa, who composed a piece of music for the concert.

8. You might be interested in an idea that Antonio had.

9. The girl whose essay won the contest was happy.

10. David crossed out each choice that was incorrect.

An adjective clause is incomplete until it is connected to at least one main clause. Even so, adjective clauses make sentences more interesting by adding important information.

> **EXAMPLE**   Mr. Ortiz found a campsite **that was available.** [The adjective clause *that was available* provides important information.]

Adjective clauses almost always have a connecting word that joins the clause to a main clause. These connecting words begin adjective clauses.

Words that Begin Adjective Clauses

that	which	who	whom	whose

EXERCISE B Underline each adjective clause in the following sentences. Then, draw an arrow from each underlined adjective clause to the noun or pronoun it describes.

Examples 1. Who are the friends to whom you sent birthday cards this year? [*To whom* begins the adjective clause. The adjective clause describes the noun *friends*.]

2. Tell me about the poem that you liked the most. [*That* begins the adjective clause. The adjective clause describes the noun *poem*.]

11. Katrina, whom I met at band camp, is marching in the parade. [Which word begins the adjective clause? Which word does the adjective clause describe?]

12. Have you seen the baseball player whose cap is on backward? [Which word begins the adjective clause? Which word does the adjective clause describe?]

13. The quizzes, which Ms. Wood will grade this afternoon, will be returned tomorrow.

14. The students will send a valentine to everyone that is in their class.

15. Sign up anyone who has a student identification card.

16. Was the player who hit the home run Shannon?

17. The hose that connected the radiator had come loose.

18. Give a program to everyone who comes in this door.

19. My parents had offered me good advice, which I followed.

20. The winner of this game is the one who gets the fewest points.

The Adverb Clause

4i. An *adverb clause* is a subordinate clause that modifies a verb, an adjective, or an adverb.

Remember that a subordinate clause does not express a complete thought and cannot stand alone. Unlike the adverb phrase, an adverb clause contains both a verb and its subject.

ADVERB **Hungrily,** the frog ate a tasty fly. [The adverb *Hungrily* describes the verb *ate.*]

ADVERB PHRASE **With a hungry gulp,** the frog ate a tasty fly. [The adverb phrase *With a hungry gulp* describes the verb *ate.*]

ADVERB CLAUSE **Because it was hungry,** the frog ate a tasty fly. [The adverb clause describes the verb *ate.* The clause has a verb, *was,* and its subject, *it.*]

Words that Commonly Begin Adverb Clauses

after	if	until
because	since	when
before	than	while

EXERCISE A The adverb clause in each of the following sentences has been underlined. Circle the word that signals the beginning of the adverb clause.

Example 1. Craig has developed some test tips so that he stays focused. [*So that* signals the beginning of the adverb clause.]

1. I wasn't hungry at lunch because I had eaten a late breakfast. [Which word signals the beginning of the adverb clause?]

2. Unless Tina knows the answer, her team will not win.

3. Before I drank the water, I squeezed a lemon into it.

4. Don't call Chen until you get home.

5. Alex closed his eyes while he thought about a topic for his paper.

6. Willis will take lessons until he joins a tennis league.

7. If you run in the relay race, will you be the first runner on your team?

8. The second loaf of bread cooked faster than the first loaf did.

9. When the light rain started, several frogs began jumping near the grassy area.

10. Candles have been providing light to the room since the power went out.

GO ON ➡

To find an adverb clause, use these questions. If you can answer *yes* to all of the following questions, you have probably found an adverb clause.

- Can you find a word that signals the beginning of an adverb clause (such as *after, before,* or *than*)?
- Do a verb and its subject follow the word?
- Does the word group describe a verb, an adjective, or an adverb?

> **EXAMPLE**   **After it flew across the pond,** the dragonfly landed on the lilypad. [*After* is a word that can signal the beginning of an adverb clause. A verb, *flew,* and its subject, *it,* follow the word *After.* The word group *After it flew across the pond* describes the verb *landed.*]

EXERCISE B   Underline the adverb clause in each of the following sentences.

Examples 1. So that our grades will improve, my friends share test tips. [*So that* signals the beginning of the adverb clause. The subject is *grades.* The verb is *will improve.*]

    2. Will you go to your grandparents' home when winter break starts? [*When* signals the beginning of the adverb clause. The subject of the clause is *break.* The verb is *starts.*]

11. While I'm visiting my cousins, we will go to a tennis tournament. [Which word group contains a word that introduces it? Does the word group contain a verb and its subject?]

12. My room will be completely clean if I spend only one hour cleaning it. [Which word group contains a word that introduces it? Does the word group contain a verb and its subject?]

13. After Lucinda studied, she took her dog Lester for a walk.

14. Please tell me about the party before you leave.

15. Unless we go to the post office now, the package will be late.

16. As long as you are going to the store, will you buy some milk?

17. We brought a sack lunch to eat while we are on the field trip.

18. Help me lift this chair so that we can move it over there.

19. Doesn't Steve write poetry when he has some spare time?

20. Before you turn in your assignment, make sure you have written your name on it.

Simple Sentences and Compound Sentences

Simple Sentences

4j.   A *simple sentence* has one independent clause and no subordinate clauses.

As you may remember, an independent clause has a subject and a verb. An independent clause expresses a complete thought and can stand alone.

V	**S**	**V**

EXAMPLES   Is Jan doing her science project? [The sentence is an independent clause.

The subject, *Jan*, comes between the parts of the verb *Is doing*.]

V

Read this newspaper article about tigers. [The sentence is an independent

clause. The subject is understood to be *you*, and the verb is *Read*.]

EXERCISE A Draw one line under the subject and two lines under the verb in each of the following sentences.

Example 1. Like her father, my <u>aunt</u> <u>is</u> a pilot. [The subject is *aunt*, and the verb is *is*.]

1. Aunt Leona has worked as a pilot for fifteen years. [Which words make up the subject? Which words make up the verb?]

2. As a teenager, she dreamed of a future in the sky.

3. With her goals in mind, she saved money.

4. Later, Aunt Leona paid for her own flying lessons.

5. Have you ever traveled in a plane or jet?

A simple sentence may have a compound subject, a compound verb, or both.

S   **S**   **V**

EXAMPLES   **Fish** and **tadpoles swam** nearby. [*Fish* and *tadpoles* make up the compound subject.]

S   **V**   **V**

Several **deer came** to the pond and **drank.** [*Came* and *drank* make up the compound verb.]

S   **S**   **V**   **V**

A **mockingbird** and her **mate were flying** overhead and **singing.**

[*Mockingbird* and *mate* make up the compound subject. *Were flying* and *singing* make up the compound verb.]

EXERCISE B Draw one line under the subject and two lines under the verb in each of the following sentences. If the subject is understood *you*, write *(you)* after the sentence. Hint: Some sentences have a compound subject, a compound verb, or both.

GO ON

Example   **1.** Has Luisa gone to the basketball court or stayed at home? [*Has gone* and *stayed* make up the compound verb.]

6. The librarian and the teacher are showing a video in the library. [Which words make up the compound subject or verb?]

7. In the evening, Cedric reads a book or writes in his journal.

8. Please call Samantha and ask her to join our team.

9. Alfredo and his brother stood in front of the building.

10. Did you walk the dog and give him a bath?

Compound Sentences

4k. A ***compound sentence*** consists of two or more independent clauses, usually joined by a comma and a connecting word.

In a compound sentence, a word such as *and, but, for, nor, or, so,* or *yet* usually connects the independent clauses. A comma usually comes before the connecting word.

> **EXAMPLES**   We had sandwiches for lunch**, and** we had fish for dinner. [The word *and* connects the two independent clauses. A comma comes before the connecting word.]
>
> I tried to reach Yoko**, but** she was not at home. [The word *but* connects the two independent clauses. A comma comes before the connecting word.]

Sometimes the independent clauses in a compound sentence are joined by a semicolon (;).

> **EXAMPLES**   These ants are called fire ants**;** their bite is painful. [The two independent clauses are joined by a semicolon.]
>
> Blanca went outside**;** she carried the basket with her. [The two independent clauses are joined by a semicolon.]

EXERCISE C   Draw one line under every independent clause in each sentence. Then, write *S* for *simple sentence* or *CD* for *compound sentence* on the line provided.

Example   *CD*   **1.** You might help a neighbor, or you might volunteer at a library. [Two independent clauses are joined by a comma and the connecting word *or*.]

_______ **11.** Carlos volunteers at the library, and he goes there once a week. [Does this sentence contain one independent clause or more than one?]

_______ **12.** Does he help out with Story Hour each Saturday afternoon?

_______ **13.** Many young children attend, for they enjoy a good tale.

_______ **14.** Watch the children's faces; they are very funny.

_______ **15.** They laugh and scream with delight at the stories.

Complex Sentences and Compound-Complex Sentences

Complex Sentences

4l. A ***complex sentence*** contains one independent clause and at least one subordinate clause.

An independent clause is a word group that contains a verb and its subject. An independent clause expresses a complete thought. A subordinate clause contains a verb and its subject, but a subordinate clause does not express a complete thought. Subordinate clauses usually begin with a word such as *who, whose, which, that, after, because, as, if, since,* or *when.* A subordinate clause can come at the beginning, in the middle, or at the end of the sentence.

	S V
INDEPENDENT CLAUSE	**she will tell** it to no one [This word group has a subject and a verb, and it expresses a complete thought.]
SUBORDINATE CLAUSE	if **you tell** Dena a secret [This word group has a subject and a verb, but it does not express a complete thought.]
COMPLEX SENTENCE	If you tell Dena a secret, she will tell it to no one. [This word group is a complex sentence. It contains an independent clause and a subordinate clause.]
INDEPENDENT CLAUSE	The **fans cheered** [This word group has a subject and a verb, and it expresses a complete thought.]
SUBORDINATE CLAUSE	when **David crossed** the finish line [This word group has a subject and a verb, but it does not express a complete thought.]
COMPLEX SENTENCE	The fans cheered when David crossed the finish line. [This word group is a complex sentence. It contains an independent clause and a subordinate clause.]

EXERCISE A The following sentences are complex sentences. Draw one line under each independent clause and draw two lines under each subordinate clause in each sentence.

Example 1. Dogs, which many people adore, are loyal and loving. [This complex sentence has one independent clause and one subordinate clause.]

1. Spiffy, who is a golden retriever, is always cheerful. [Which part of the sentence expresses a complete thought? Which part does not express a complete thought?]

2. He greets me joyfully at the door as soon as I get home.

3. I usually play with him in the yard after I put my backpack in my room.

4. Before he will catch the ball, Spiffy likes to run around the yard a few times.

5. Spiffy always jumps high whenever I throw the ball.

GO ON

Compound-Complex Sentences

4m. A sentence with two or more independent clauses and at least one subordinate clause is a *compound-complex sentence.*

                     S   V

INDEPENDENT CLAUSE **Ashley read** a magazine [This word group has a subject and a verb, and it expresses a complete thought.]

                     S   V

INDEPENDENT CLAUSE **Andy played** his guitar [This word group has a subject and a verb, and it expresses a complete thought.]

                    S   V

SUBORDINATE CLAUSE that **she had bought** [This word group has a subject and a verb, but it does not express a complete thought.]

COMPOUND-COMPLEX   S   V   S   V   S   V
      SENTENCE **Ashley read** a magazine that **she had bought**, and **Andy played** his guitar.

[This word group is a compound-complex sentence. It contains two independent clauses and one subordinate clause.]

EXERCISE B Identify each of the following sentences by writing *CX* for *complex* or *CD-CX* for *compound-complex*. Write your answer on the line provided. Hint: A complex sentence has only one independent clause; a compound-complex sentence has at least two independent clauses.

Example _CD-CX_ **1.** I wrote a note to a friend who was feeling sick, and I put it on his desk.

[This word group contains two independent clauses, *I wrote a note to a friend* and *I put it on his desk,* and one subordinate clause, *who was feeling sick.* Therefore, the word group is a compound-complex sentence.]

_______ **6.** Did I hear the doorbell, or was it the telephone that rang? [How many independent clauses are there in this sentence?]

_______ **7.** When Diane was in San Francisco, she snapped a photo of the Golden Gate Bridge, for she collects photos of bridges.

_______ **8.** Set up the volleyball for Paula, who will spike it over the net.

_______ **9.** The cold river, which is in the valley between two mountains, rushed over the rocks.

_______ **10.** The sixth-graders, who are raising money for a field trip, are holding a bake sale, and they need your help.

Direct Objects and Indirect Objects

Direct Objects

5b. A *direct object* is a noun, pronoun, or word group that tells who or what receives the action of the verb.

Every sentence has a subject and a verb. Some sentences have a *direct object,* which receives the action of the verb. To find a direct object, ask the question *Whom?* or *What?* after the subject and the verb. A direct object is the word or word group that answers this question.

DIRECT OBJECTS Rosie's grandmother hugged **her.** [Rosie's grandmother hugged *whom?* Hugged *her.* The direct object *her* receives the action of the verb *hugged.*]

Did Mary read **The Call of the Wild** last summer? [Did Mary read *what?* Did read *The Call of the Wild.* The direct object *The Call of the Wild* receives the action of the verb *read.*]

EXERCISE A Circle the direct object in each of the following sentences. Hint: The subject and the verb of each sentence have been underlined for you.

Example 1. Just before take-off, the pilot gave an (announcement) to the passengers. [The verb of the sentence is *gave.* The answer to the question *The pilot gave* what? is an announcement. *Announcement* is the direct object.]

1. The hammer drove the nail into the plywood. [Which word is the verb in this sentence? Which word receives the action of the verb?]

2. My uncle visited Miami last year.

3. The youth group cleaned the shed for Mrs. Nelson.

4. May I pay the bill with a check?

5. In her younger days, my grandmother won many swimming contests.

NOTE▶ Not every sentence has a direct object. A direct object can never follow a verb that does not express action.

NO DIRECT OBJECT Haley **seemed** happy. [The verb *seemed* does not express an action. There is no direct object in the sentence.]

DIRECT OBJECT Haley **kicked** the soccer ball. [The verb *kicked* does express an action. The ball received the kick, so *ball* is the direct object.]

A sentence may have more than one direct object. Two or more direct objects that complete the meaning of the same verb are called a *compound direct object.*

EXAMPLE Nadine has invited **Phil, Maria,** and **Siri** to the movies. [Nadine invited *whom?* Invited *Phil, Maria,* and *Siri.* The names *Phil, Maria,* and *Siri* make up the compound direct object of *has invited.*]

GO ON ▶

EXERCISE B Underline each direct object in the following sentences. One sentence has a compound direct object.

Example 1. Lupita had a creative idea for her class. [The answer to the question *Had what?* is *idea*. The word *idea* completes the meaning of the verb *had*. *Idea* is the direct object.]

6. The sixth-graders were making posters. [The sixth-graders were making *what?*]

7. Lupita was using special tape.

8. First, she stuck the tape onto her poster.

9. Next, she pulled the backing from the other side of the tape.

10. Finally, she sprinkled beads and glitter onto the sticky surface.

Indirect Objects

5c. An ***indirect object*** is a noun, pronoun, or word group that usually comes between the verb and the direct object. An indirect object tells *to whom* or *to what* or *for whom* or *for what* the action of the verb is done.

                IO   DO

EXAMPLES Feed the **calf** its dinner. [The noun *calf* is the indirect object of the verb *Feed*. *Calf* answers the question "*To what* was dinner fed?"]

                IO   DO

The principal gave **Mrs. Diaz** an award. [The compound noun *Mrs. Diaz* is the indirect object of the verb *gave*. *Mrs. Diaz* answers the question "*To whom* did the principal give an award?"]

Like a direct object, an indirect object can be compound.

           IO   IO   DO

EXAMPLE Jill sent **Pedro** and **Adam** e-mails. [*Pedro* and *Adam* are indirect objects of the verb *sent*. They answer the question "*To whom* did Jill send e-mails?"]

EXERCISE C Circle each indirect object in the following sentences. One sentence has a compound indirect object. Hint: The direct objects have been underlined for you.

Example 1. At the garage sale, Mark sold his (neighbor) a table and four chairs. [The *neighbor* is the person to whom the table and chairs were sold. *Neighbor* is the indirect object.]

11. Please show me your new outfit. [Who is the person the new outfit is being shown to?]

12. The counselor told the campers some important advice.

13. Kris has given the bookshelf a new coat of paint.

14. After the game, the team promised itself and its fans a victory party.

15. Did the waiter bring you that menu?

Predicate Nominatives and Predicate Adjectives

Predicate Nominatives

5e. A *predicate nominative* is a word or word group that is in the predicate and that identifies the subject or refers to it.

A predicate nominative is usually a noun or pronoun. A predicate nominative is always connected to the subject by a linking verb.

                                        S   PN
EXAMPLES Is Daniel's favorite game **chess**? [The noun *chess* is a predicate nominative. *Chess* follows the linking verb *Is* and identifies the subject *game*.]

                         S   PN
The book on the shelf was **Alice's Adventures in Wonderland.** [The word group *Alice's Adventures in Wonderland* is a predicate nominative. The book title follows the linking verb *was* and identifies the subject *book*.]

REMINDER Some common linking verbs are *appear, be, become, feel, grow, look, remain, seem, smell, sound, stay,* and *taste.*

EXERCISE A Circle the predicate nominative in each of the following sentences. Hint: The predicate has already been underlined for you.

Example 1. Will Ruth become the (treasurer) of the sixth-grade class? [The word *treasurer* follows the linking verb *Will become* and identifies the subject *Ruth,* so *treasurer* is the predicate nominative.]

1. The leader of the food drive is Amanda. [Which word identifies the subject *leader*?]

2. Was the dog in that commercial a collie?

3. My favorite color is green.

4. Last year, the organizer of the book fair was Leena Benson.

5. That tall building is the Empire State Building.

Predicate Adjectives

5f. A *predicate adjective* is an adjective that is in the predicate and that describes the subject.

Like a predicate nominative, a *predicate adjective* is connected to the subject by a linking verb. Instead of identifying the subject, though, a predicate adjective describes the subject.

                              S   PA
EXAMPLES The patient's heartbeat is **strong.** [The adjective *strong* describes the subject *heartbeat.*]

                    S   PA
Her tennis serve is especially **fast.** [The adjective *fast* describes the subject *serve.* The word *especially* describes *fast,* not the subject *serve.*

GO ON

Especially is not part of the predicate adjective.]

EXERCISE B Circle the predicate adjective in each of the following sentences. Hint: The predicate has already been underlined for you.

Example 1. Did Randy appear happy? [The word *happy* describes the subject *Randy*, so *happy* is the predicate adjective.]

6. These roses smell sweet. [Which word in the underlined section describes the subject *roses*?]

7. My sister stays calm in a crisis.

8. Are the floors wet from the detergent?

9. One actor looked nervous.

10. The soup at the restaurant was too hot.

Predicate nominatives and predicate adjectives may be compound.

                      S   **PN**   **PN**   **PN**

PREDICATE NOMINATIVE Are the ingredients **green peppers, garlic,** and **vinegar?** [*Green peppers, garlic,* and *vinegar* make up a compound predicate nominative. They identify the subject *ingredients* and complete the meaning of the linking verb *Are.*]

                      S   **PA**   **PA**

PREDICATE ADJECTIVE In the cold weather, the horses grew **playful** and **energetic.** [The adjectives *playful* and *energetic* describe the subject *horses*. These words make up a compound predicate adjective. They complete the meaning of the linking verb *grew.*]

EXERCISE C The underlined words in the sentences below are compound subject complements. Write *PN* on the line provided if the underlined words are *predicate nominatives,* or write *PA* if they are *predicate adjectives.*

Example _PA_ **1.** After our long day at the fair, we looked sleepy yet happy. [The words *sleepy* and *happy* describe the subject *we*. These words are the predicate adjective.]

_______ **11.** Was the winner of the prize your aunt or your uncle? [Do the words *aunt* and *uncle* describe the subject *winner*? Do they identify the subject *winner* instead?]

_______ **12.** The fairgrounds were bright and attractive.

_______ **13.** Our snack was peanuts and juice.

_______ **14.** The line for the bumper cars was long and slow.

_______ **15.** Are the three people in the background Tim Vinson, Ed Garcia, and Cindy Spencer?

Subject-Verb Agreement

6b.   A verb should agree in number with its subject.

A subject and verb agree when they have the same number. When a word refers to one person, place, thing, or idea, it is *singular* in number. When a word refers to more than one person, place, thing, or idea, it is *plural* in number.

Singular Verbs

(1) Singular subjects take singular verbs.

Most verbs that end in *–s*, such as *does* or *stops*, are singular.

> S   V
> **EXAMPLES**   The **flower dries** in the heat. [The singular verb *dries* agrees with the singular subject *flower.*]
>
> S   V
> Our **uncle owns** a car repair shop. [The singular verb *owns* agrees with the singular subject *uncle.*]

NOTE▶ Verbs used with the singular pronouns *I* and *you* usually do not end in *–s*.

> S V
> **EXAMPLES**   **I watch** the news every day. [The singular verb *watch*, which does not end in *–s*, agrees with the singular pronoun *I*.]
>
> S   V
> **You need** your library card today. [The singular verb *need*, which does not end in *–s*, agrees with the singular pronoun *You*.]

EXERCISE A   Circle the verb in parentheses that agrees with the subject in each of the following sentences.

Example 1. My brother *(want,* (*wants*)*)* a new bicycle. [The subject, *brother*, is singular, so the verb must be singular, too.]

1. The bus *(stops, stop)* in front of my house. [Is the subject singular or plural?]

2. I *(make, makes)* my own lunch every day.

3. The dog *(sleeps, sleep)* on the floor in the kitchen.

4. You *(brings, bring)* the rake and the shovel.

5. Kate *(hangs, hang)* her coat in the closet.

Plural Verbs

(2) Plural subjects take plural verbs.

> S   V
> **EXAMPLES**   **Students write** many essays. [The plural verb *write* agrees with the plural subject *Students.*]

GO ON ➡

>   S   V
>
> Many **stars shine** in the night sky. [The plural verb *shine* agrees with the
>
> plural subject *stars*.]

EXERCISE B Circle the verb form that agrees with the subject in each of the following sentences.

Example 1. Many people (*has,* have) nicknames. [The subject *people* is plural, so the verb must be

         plural, too.]

6. Nicknames sometimes (*comes, come*) from given names. [Is the subject singular or plural?]

7. Some families always (*give, gives*) a son the father's first name.

8. The parents often (*uses, use*) a nickname for the son.

9. Other nicknames (*reflect, reflects*) how a person looks or acts.

10. Sometimes initials (*becomes, become*) a person's nickname.

Agreement with Helping Verbs

A *verb phrase* is made up of a main verb and one or more helping verbs. The first helping
verb in the verb phrase agrees with the subject.

        EXAMPLES   A **bird has built** a nest in our maple tree. [*Has built* is the verb phrase. The
                  singular helping verb *has* agrees with the singular subject *bird*.]
                  Some **birds have built** their nests in our maple tree. [*Have built* is the verb
                  phrase. The plural helping verb *have* agrees with the plural subject *birds*.]

REMINDER   Even when the first helping verb comes before the subject, it should agree with the
         subject.

        EXAMPLE   **Do** the **girls make** their own decorations? [*Do make* is the verb phrase. The
                  plural helping verb *Do* agrees with the plural subject *girls*.]

EXERCISE C Circle the helping verb that agrees with the subject in each of the following sentences.

Example 1. The birds (*has,* have) been flying south for weeks. [The subject *birds* is plural, so the

         helping verb must be plural, too.]

11. Five friends (*is, are*) going on a bike trip together. [Is the subject singular or plural?]

12. (*Does, Do*) Sonya have a good dictionary?

13. (*Has, Have*) you heard the good news yet?

14. (*Is, Are*) he planning his birthday party?

15. I (*has, have*) enjoyed our unit on film history.

Subject-Verb Agreement: Indefinite Pronouns

A pronoun that does not refer to a specific person, place, thing, or idea is called an *indefinite pronoun.* When an indefinite pronoun is used as a subject, make sure the verb agrees with the pronoun.

Singular Indefinite Pronouns

6d. Use a singular verb to agree with the following pronouns when they are used as subjects:

anybody	either	neither	one
anyone	everybody	nobody	somebody
anything	everyone	no one	someone
each	everything	nothing	something

EXAMPLES **Everyone brings** lunch to school. [The singular verb *brings* agrees in number with the singular subject *Everyone.*]

One of the boys **eats** his broccoli. [The singular verb *eats* agrees with the singular subject *One.*]

NOTE▶ Many indefinite pronouns can also be used as adjectives. When these words are used as adjectives, they do not affect the number of the verb.

ADJECTIVE **Each** student needs a book. [The adjective *Each* is an adjective that modifies the noun *student. Student* is the subject of the verb *needs.*]

EXERCISE A Circle the verb in parentheses that agrees with the subject in each of the following sentences. Each subject has been underlined for you.

Example 1. Everyone *(know,* (*knows*)) the importance of good dental care. [The indefinite pronoun *Everyone* is always singular, so the verb should be singular, too.]

1. Anything *(is, are)* fine for lunch today. [Is the indefinite pronoun *Anything* always singular?]

2. Neither of the desserts *(contain, contains)* sugar.

3. Everybody on the team *(has, have)* new equipment.

4. Anyone with extra time *(help, helps)* out in the library.

5. Almost no one *(wakes, wake)* up that early!

Plural Indefinite Pronouns

6e. Use a plural verb to agree with the following pronouns when they are used as subjects:

both	few	many	several

EXAMPLE **Many** of the forecasts **predict** rain. [The plural verb *predict* agrees with the plural subject *Many.*]

GO ON ➡

EXERCISE B Circle the verb in parentheses that agrees with the subject in each of the following sentences. Each subject has been underlined for you.

Example 1. Several of these ingredients (*tastes,* *taste*) good. [The indefinite pronoun *Several* is

always plural, so the verb should be plural, too.]

6. Few of my friends (*has, have*) seen that movie. [Is the indefinite pronoun *Few* always plural?]

7. Both of the doors (*locks, lock*) securely.

8. Several of the paintings (*hang, hangs*) in the museum.

9. Many (*have, has*) beautiful frames.

10. Few of the rosebushes (*is, are*) blooming yet.

Singular or Plural Indefinite Pronouns

6f.   The following indefinite pronouns may be singular or plural, depending on how they are used in a sentence:

| all | any | more | most | none | some |

Look at the phrase that follows the indefinite pronoun. If the noun in that phrase is singular, the pronoun is singular, too. If the noun in that phrase is plural, the pronoun is plural, too.

EXAMPLES **All** of the **exercise was** challenging. [The subject *All* is singular because it refers to the singular noun *exercise*. The singular verb *was* agrees with the singular subject *All*.]

All of the **exercises were** challenging. [The subject *All* is plural because it refers to the plural noun *exercises*. The plural verb *were* agrees with the plural subject *All*.]

EXERCISE C Underline the subject in each of the following sentences. Then, circle the verb in parentheses that agrees with the subject.

Example 1. Most of the children (*brushes,* *brush*) their teeth at least twice a day. [The subject is

Most. The noun in the phrase that follows the subject is the plural *children*, so *Most* is

plural, too. The plural verb *brush* agrees with the plural subject.]

11. Some of the carrots (*is, are*) already sliced. [What is the subject? Is the noun in the phrase that

follows it singular or plural? Which verb agrees with the subject?]

12. None of the test (*seems, seem*) difficult.

13. All of the apples (*tastes, taste*) delicious.

14. More of the wheat (*are, is*) stored in the grain bin.

15. Any of these books (*interest, interests*) me.

Subject-Verb Agreement: Compound Subjects

As you may remember, a *subject* tells who or what a sentence is about. Sometimes, two (or more) subjects combine to form one *compound subject.*

Subjects Joined by *And*

6g.   Subjects joined by *and* generally take a plural verb.

>   S   S   V
> **EXAMPLE**   **Sandwiches** and **soup are** both on the menu today. [*Sandwiches* and *soup* are joined by *and*. The plural verb *are* agrees with the compound subject *Sandwiches and soup.*]

REMINDER ▸ The first helping verb in a verb phrase should agree with the subject.

> **EXAMPLE**   The **rowboats and canoe are** always **stored** in that building. [*Rowboats* and *canoe* are joined by *and*. The verb phrase is *are stored*. The plural helping verb *are* agrees with the compound subject *rowboats and canoe.*]

EXERCISE A   Circle the verb in parentheses that agrees with the compound subject in each of the following sentences. Each compound subject has been underlined for you.

Example 1. Fruit and skim milk (*have*, *has*) always been two of my favorite foods. [The subjects *Fruit* and *milk* are joined by *and*, so the helping verb must be plural.]

1. Stretches and exercises (*gets*, *get*) the day going well. [Are the subjects joined by *and*?]

2. Mom and Dad (*reminds*, *remind*) us that we should not be late for school.

3. Saturdays and Sundays (*is*, *are*) good days for sleeping late.

4. (*Do*, *Does*) news and music wake you up, or does a noisy alarm buzzer?

5. Sunshine and chirping birds (*wakes*, *wake*) me up in the summer.

Subjects Joined by *Or* or *Nor*

6h.   Singular subjects that are joined by *or* or *nor* take a singular verb.

6i.   Plural subjects joined by *or* or *nor* take a plural verb.

You will sometimes see the words *either* and *neither* used in combination with *or* and *nor*.

>   S   S   V
> **EXAMPLES**   **Neither thunder nor lightning bothers** our dogs. [The singular verb *bothers* agrees with the singular subject *thunder* and the singular subject *lightning.*]
>
>   S   S   V
> **Either ducks or chickens are raised** on that farm. [The plural helping verb *are* agrees with the plural subject *ducks* and the plural subject *chickens.*]

GO ON ▸

EXERCISE B Circle the verb in parentheses that agrees with the compound subject in each of the following sentences. Each compound subject has been underlined for you.

Example 1. Juice or a banana (*starts*, *start*) the morning off right. [The singular subjects *Juice* and banana are joined by *or*, so the verb must be singular, too.]

 6. Sometimes Mom or Aunt Rachel (*drive*, *drives*) me to school. [Are the subjects singular? Are the subjects joined by *or* or *nor*?]

 7. Neither my sisters nor my brothers (*stays*, *stay*) in the sun too long.

 8. (*Have*, *Has*) either the flowers or the shrubs been planted yet?

 9. Either the bat or the ball (*belong*, *belongs*) to him.

 10. (*Do*, *Does*) either Kristen or Mike have an extra pencil?

Singular and Plural Subjects Joined by *Or* or *Nor*

6j. When a singular subject and a plural subject are joined by *or* or *nor*, the verb agrees with the subject nearer to the verb.

	S	S	V

EXAMPLES Either the **slide** or the **swings were removed.** [The plural subject *swings* is nearer to the helping verb *were*. The plural verb *were* agrees with the plural subject *swings*.]

Either the **swings** or the **slide was removed.** [The singular subject *slide* is nearer to the helping verb *was*. The singular verb *was* agrees with the singular subject *slide*.]

EXERCISE C Circle the verb in parentheses that agrees with the compound subject in each of the following sentences. Each compound subject has been underlined for you.

Example 1. Neither April nor her cousins (*has*, *have*) visited the zoo. [The plural subject *cousins* is nearer to the verb, so the verb must be plural.]

 11. Either a salad or two vegetables (*comes*, *come*) with every meal. [Is the subject that is nearer the verb singular or plural?]

 12. Neither his notes nor the book (*was*, *were*) returned.

 13. Two pieces of toast or a bowl of cereal (*is*, *are*) all I want.

 14. Kevin or his younger sisters (*clears*, *clear*) the table after dinner.

 15. Neither her jacket nor her boots (*was*, *were*) in the closet.

Pronoun-Antecedent Agreement A

A *pronoun* is a word that takes the place of a noun or another pronoun. The word a pronoun replaces is called the pronoun's *antecedent.*

Agreement in Gender

6n. A pronoun should agree in gender with its antecedent.

Some singular pronouns have forms that tell the gender of the person or thing the pronoun replaces. Feminine pronouns (*she, her, hers,* and *herself*) refer to females. Masculine pronouns (*he, him, his, himself*) refer to males. Neuter pronouns (*it, it, its, itself*) refer to things that are neither female nor male. Neuter pronouns also sometimes refer to animals.

> **EXAMPLES**   The **lioness** groomed **her** coat. [The feminine pronoun *her* agrees with its feminine antecedent, the noun *lioness.*]
>
> My **brother** was putting on **his** football pads. [The masculine pronoun *his* agrees with its masculine antecedent, the noun *brother.*]
>
> The **horse** ate from **its** feedbag. [The neuter pronoun *its* agrees with its neuter antecedent, the noun *horse.*]

EXERCISE A Circle the pronoun in parentheses that agrees with the antecedent in each of the following sentences. Each antecedent has been underlined for you.

Example 1. My <u>brother</u> wants to know the meaning of (**his**, *her, its*) name. [The antecedent is the masculine noun *brother,* so the pronoun must be masculine, too.]

1. Then my <u>sister</u> asked about (*his, her, its*) name, Katherine. [Is the antecedent masculine, feminine, or neuter?]

2. My <u>father</u> was named after (*his, her, its*) grandfather.

3. <u>Dad</u> says that (*he, she, it*) wants a new car next year.

4. I can't find my <u>jacket</u> because I didn't put (*him, her, it*) away.

5. The <u>mother bear</u> defended (*his, her, its*) cubs.

Agreement in Number

6o. A pronoun should agree with its antecedent in number.

A pronoun that has a singular antecedent should be singular in number. A pronoun that has a plural antecedent should be plural in number.

> **EXAMPLES**   Please put the **dishes** away after you wash **them.** [The antecedent of the pronoun is the plural noun *dishes.* The plural pronoun *them* agrees in number with the plural noun *dishes.*]
>
> May I read that **book** after you finish **it?** [The antecedent of the pronoun is the singular noun *book.* The singular pronoun *it* agrees in number with the singular noun *book.*]

GO ON

for **CHAPTER 6: AGREEMENT**   **pages 183–186** *continued*

NOTE▶ Plural pronouns do not show gender.

> **EXAMPLE** The **girls** tied **their** shoes. [The plural pronoun *their* agrees in number with its antecedent, the plural noun *girls*. The pronoun does not have to agree in gender because plural pronouns do not show gender.]

EXERCISE B Circle the pronoun in parentheses that agrees in number with the antecedent. Each antecedent has been underlined for you.

Example 1. The birds carried twigs for *(its,* **their** *)* nest. [The plural noun *birds* is the antecedent of the pronoun. The antecedent is plural, so the pronoun must be plural, too.]

6. The patient spider waited for *(their, its)* prey. [Is the antecedent singular or plural?]

7. She bought new shoes, but she hasn't worn *(them, it)* yet.

8. I once knew all the words of that song, but I don't remember *(them, it)* all now.

9. The children needed a ball for *(their, its)* game.

10. The dog is not afraid of cats, but it barks at *(them, it)* a lot.

Agreement with Compound Antecedents

Use a plural pronoun to refer to two or more antecedents joined by *and.*

> **EXAMPLE** Both the **girls** and the **boys** like **their** new teacher. [*Girls* and *boys* are joined by *and*. The pronoun that refers to *girls and boys* is plural.]

Use a singular pronoun to refer to two or more singular antecedents joined by *or* or *nor.*

> **EXAMPLE** Neither **Sara** nor **Karen** braids **her** hair anymore. [The antecedents, *Sara* and *Karen*, are both singular and feminine. The singular feminine pronoun *her* agrees with *Sara* and with *Karen*.]

EXERCISE C Circle the pronoun in parentheses that agrees with the compound antecedent in each of the sentences below. Each antecedent has been underlined for you.

Example 1. Neither her aunt nor her mother brought *(their,* **her** *)* wallet. [The antecedents *aunt* and *mother* are singular, feminine nouns joined by *nor*. The pronoun must also be singular and feminine.]

11. Both Carl and his brothers work for *(their, his)* spending money. [Are the antecedents singular or plural? What word joins the antecedents? Does the gender of the antecedents make any difference?]

12. I don't remember whether bees or wasps build *(their, its)* nests in trees.

13. Either Mary or Katie will bring *(their, her)* guitar to the party.

14. Mary and Katie will sing *(their, her)* favorite song.

15. Neither the dog nor the cat will eat *(their, its)* food tonight.

for **CHAPTER 6: AGREEMENT** | **pages 184–186**

Pronoun-Antecedent Agreement B

6o. A pronoun should agree with its antecedent in number.

Singular Indefinite Pronouns

A pronoun that does not refer to a specific person, place, thing, or idea is called an *indefinite pronoun.*

Use a singular pronoun to refer to the following indefinite pronouns:

anybody	either	neither	one
anyone	everybody	nobody	somebody
anything	everyone	no one	someone
each	everything	nothing	something

> **EXAMPLE** Did **anyone** forget to bring **his or her** permission slip? [*His or her* agrees in number with the antecedent *anyone,* because *anyone* is always singular and *his* and *her* are both singular. In this sentence, *anyone* may include both males and females.]

EXERCISE A Circle the pronoun in parentheses that agrees with the antecedent in each of the following sentences. Each antecedent has been underlined for you.

Example 1. Everybody knows that *(he or she, they)* should eat lots of vegetables. [*Everybody* is a singular indefinite pronoun, so the antecedent must be singular, too.]

1. Each of the cats cleans *(its, their)* fur carefully. [Is the antecedent singular or plural?]

2. No one will fail to do *(his or her, their)* best today.

3. Something made *(his or her, its)* presence known in the room.

4. Will somebody please lend *(his or her, their)* book to Leo?

5. One of those young men will win *(his, their)* race today.

Plural Indefinite Pronouns

Use a plural pronoun to refer to the following indefinite pronouns:

both	few	many	several

> **EXAMPLE** **Few** of the teams have **their** own buses. [The plural pronoun *their* agrees with the plural antecedent *Few.*]

EXERCISE B Circle the pronoun in parentheses that agrees with the antecedent in each of the following sentences. Each antecedent has been underlined for you.

Example 1. Several of the model airplanes have *(its, their)* original paint. [The indefinite pronoun *Several* is always plural, so the pronoun must be plural, too.]

GO ON

6. Both of my sister's dolls have (*its, their*) special places on a shelf. [Is the antecedent singular or plural?]

7. Few of these old stamps have glue on (*its, their*) backs.

8. Many of my friends have started (*his or her, their*) own collections.

9. Several of the collections have cost (*its, their*) owners a lot of time and money.

10. Do many of your friends remember (*his or her, their*) first hobbies?

Singular or Plural Indefinite Pronouns

The following indefinite pronouns may be singular or plural, depending on how they are used in a sentence:

all	any	more	most	none	some

Look at the phrase following the indefinite pronoun. If the noun in that phrase is singular, the pronoun should be singular, too. If the noun in that phrase in plural, the pronoun should be plural, too.

> **EXAMPLES** **Most** of the **building** had lost **its** roof in the tornado. [The indefinite pronoun *Most* is singular because *building*, the noun in the phrase that follows the antecedent, is singular. The singular pronoun *its* agrees with the singular antecedent *Most*.]
>
> **Most** of the **windows** had lost **their** glass in the tornado. [The indefinite pronoun *Most* is plural because *windows*, the noun in the phrase that follows the antecedent, is plural. The plural pronoun *their* agrees with the plural antecedent *Most*.]

EXERCISE C In each of the following sentences, the antecedent has been underlined for you. First, underline the word in the phrase following the antecedent that will tell you whether the antecedent is singular or plural. Then, circle the pronoun in parentheses that agrees with the antecedent.

Example 1. All of Ann's collection is in (*its* *their*) protective box. [The word *collection*, in the phrase following the antecedent, is singular and neuter.]

11. Most of my baseball cards have kept (*its, their*) value. [Is the noun that follows the antecedent singular or plural?]

12. Most of this metal box has rust on (*it, them*).

13. Have some of your old coins lost (*its, their*) shine?

14. Any of these nickels will shine if you polish (*it, them*).

15. Does any of the bread have oats in (*it, them*)?

Principal Parts of Verbs

7a. The four principal parts of a verb are the ***base form,*** the ***present participle,*** the ***past,*** and the ***past participle.***

BASE FORM	PRESENT PARTICIPLE	PAST	PAST PARTICIPLE
walk	[is] walking	walked	[have] walked
ring	[is] ringing	rang	[have] rung

NOTE The words *is* and *have* are included in this chart because present participle and past participle verb forms need helping verbs (forms of *be* and *have*) to form verb tenses.

EXERCISE A Identify the form of the underlined verb in each of the following sentences. Write *base form, present participle, past,* or *past participle* on the lines provided.

Examples __*past participle*__ **1.** The printer paper has <u>jammed</u> again. [*Jammed* is the past participle of the verb *jam.*]

__*present participle*__ **2.** Are you <u>buying</u> more paper? [*Buying* is the present participle of the verb *buy.*]

______________ **1.** On that day, we <u>played</u> the hardest doubles match yet. [Which principal part of the verb *play* is the underlined word?]

______________ **2.** Has Shannon <u>written</u> her thank-you notes yet? [Which principal part of the verb *write* is the underlined word?]

______________ **3.** When we <u>closed</u> the door, the rain couldn't get in.

______________ **4.** The baby is <u>fussing</u> because he is tired.

______________ **5.** The matinee movie has already <u>begun</u>.

______________ **6.** We silently watched the choir <u>sing</u> the song with great emotion.

______________ **7.** The painters have <u>finished</u> the outside of the house.

______________ **8.** The weather is <u>changing</u> from warm and dry to cool and wet.

______________ **9.** Our breath <u>showed</u> up as frost on the window on that cold afternoon.

______________ **10.** I saw Danny <u>ride</u> the bus to school this morning.

GO ON

A verb that forms its past and past participle by adding *–d* or *–ed* is called a regular verb. A verb that forms its past and past participle differently is called an irregular verb.

> **EXAMPLES**   Bianca **helped** her mother with the infant. [*Helped* is the past form of the verb *help*. *Helped* ends in *–ed* and is a regular past form.]
>
>   The shopkeeper **thought** that it was time to close. [*Thought* is the past form of the verb *think*. *Thought* is irregular.]
>
>   Has the bell **rung** yet? [*Rung* is the past participle form of the verb *ring*. *Rung* is irregular.]

EXERCISE B   Underline the correct verb form in parentheses in each of the following sentences.

Examples 1. Kite day at school is (come, *coming*) up soon! [*Coming* is the present participle of the verb *come*.]

          2. Have you (*built*, builded) your kite yet? [*Built* is the past participle of the verb *build*.]

11. Last year I (*winned*, *won*) the prize for the smallest kite that flew. [Which word in parentheses is the correct past form of *win*?]

12. My kite (*measure*, *measured*) three inches tall and two inches wide. [Which word in parentheses is the correct past form of *measure*?]

13. I (*coloring*, *colored*) it bright red so that I could see it against the sky.

14. Many people have (*known*, *know*) how to build a kite since they were children.

15. We are (*plan*, *planning*) for a large, flat kite with a cloth tail.

16. My class (*studied*, *studying*) the math behind kites and how they fly.

17. A tail (*help*, *helped*) my tiny kite fly.

18. We are (*adding*, *add*) longer tails to balance our kites.

19. This year I am (*built*, *building*) a really big kite!

20. I have (*using*, *used*) my math and geometry to design it so that it will fly high.

Regular Verbs

7b.   A regular verb forms its past and past participle by adding *–d* or *–ed* to the base form.

BASE FORM OF VERB	PRESENT PARTICIPLE (*–ING* FORM)	PAST FORM (*–ED* FORM)	PAST PARTICIPLE (*–ED* FORM)
listen	[is] listening	listened	[have] listened
cook	[is] cooking	cooked	[have] cooked
visit	[is] visiting	visited	[have] visited

TIP When people speak quickly, they sometimes sound as though they are dropping the *–d* or *–ed* ending, especially in words like *used, supposed,* and *prejudiced.* Keep in mind that, no matter how these words sound, they end in *–ed.* Make sure that you write these words correctly.

NONSTANDARD   Cynthia use to do gymnastics in elementary school.

STANDARD   Cynthia **used** to do gymnastics in elementary school. [The past form of the verb *use* ends in *–d, used.*]

EXERCISE A   Underline the correct verb form in parentheses in each of the following sentences.

Examples 1. I never (*realize, realized*) before how beautiful that picture was. [The correct past form of *realize* is *realized.*]

2. Are the children (*laughed, laughing*) at the funny video? [The correct present participle form of *laugh* is *laughing.*]

1. Our team has (*place, placed*) first in its division for the last three years. [Which word is the correct past participle form of *place*?]

2. The constant drip of the faucet is (*bothered, bothering*) me. [Which word is the correct present participle form of *bother*?]

3. Are we (*suppose, supposed*) to turn in our assignments today or tomorrow?

4. I have always (*like, liked*) to play the piano.

5. In the school's library, Luis (*research, researched*) his essay topic.

6. Kay has often (*dreaming, dreamed*) about herself as a child.

7. The key to the door (*remained, remain*) lost.

8. Luisa (*used, use*) to attend Johnson Middle School.

9. Have you (*deciding, decided*) where to hang your new posters?

10. All of the other students are (*watched, watching*) the soccer game.

GO ON

Before adding an *–ing* or *–ed* to a verb that ends in an *–e*, you usually need to drop the *–e*.

> **EXAMPLES** use **us**ing **us**ed
>
> live **liv**ing **liv**ed

Before adding an *–ing* or *–ed* to a verb that ends in a consonant, you sometimes need to double the consonant.

> **EXAMPLES** clap **clapp**ing **clapp**ed
>
> stop **stopp**ing **stopp**ed

Before adding an *–ed* to a verb that ends in *–y*, you usually need to change the *y* to an *i*.

> **EXAMPLES** hurry + ed = hurr**i**ed
>
> marry + ed = marr**i**ed

EXERCISE B Fill in the blank in each sentence with the correct form of the regular verb. The verb you will use is given in parentheses after each sentence.

Examples 1. Is Dad ___*chopping*___ the vegetables? (chop + ing) [The final consonant of the verb

chop must be doubled to form the present participle *chopping*.]

2. The baby has ___*cried*___ all night long. (cry + ed) [The *y* in the verb *cry* must

change to *i* to form the past participle *cried*.]

11. The children ___________ along the sidewalk. (skip + ed) [Should the final consonant of the

verb *skip* be doubled?]

12. Have you ever ___________ the exercises shown in this book? (try + ed) [Should the *y* in *try* be

changed to an *i*?]

13. Our family is ___________ to go on a nice vacation this year. (hope + ing)

14. We are all ___________ to help with the chores today. (suppose + ed)

15. The meeting ___________ late in the day. (occur + ed)

16. Weren't you ___________ by the news? (stun + ed)

17. The city is now ___________ all plastic and glass materials. (recycle + ing)

18. The committee has ___________ out a solution to the problem. (map + ed)

19. Are the managers ___________ the employees with lunch? (provide + ing)

20. The horse slowly ___________ across the meadow. (trot + ed)

Irregular Verbs A

7c. An ***irregular verb*** forms its past and past participle in some other way than by adding –*d* or –*ed* to the base form.

Some irregular verbs make their past and past participle forms by changing consonants. Here are some common irregular verbs that change consonants in their past forms. Read these verbs aloud slowly. Become familiar with how they sound and how they look.

BASE FORM	PAST	PAST PARTICIPLE
have	had	[have] had
hear	heard	[have] heard
lend	lent	[have] lent
lose	lost	[have] lost
make	made	[have] made
send	sent	[have] sent
spend	spent	[have] spent

TIP Irregular verbs do not follow an easy pattern like the –*ed* pattern of regular verbs. If you are not sure how to make an irregular verb's past forms, look the verb up in a current dictionary.

REMINDER Irregular verbs form their –*ing* form just as regular verbs do.

EXAMPLE　The choir is **singing** the school song.

EXERCISE A Underline the correct form of the irregular verb in parentheses in each of the following sentences.

Examples 1. Have you (*sended, sent*) the letter yet? [The correct form of the past participle of the verb *send* is *sent*.]

2. I already (*heared, heard*) the news. [The correct past form of the verb *hear* is *heard*.]

1. The public library (*lended, lent*) me this book. [Which word is the correct past form of the verb *lend*?]

2. Has the dog (*had, haved*) its supper yet? [Which word is the correct form of the past participle of the verb *have*?]

3. Our team (*made, maked*) a perfect score.

4. Marco said that he (*spended, spent*) a lot of time working in the garden.

5. I have (*lost, losed*) my keys!

6. The cat (*heard, heared*) the cricket under the rug.

7. Samuel has (*lent, lended*) me a hand with this job.

8. Last Friday, our football team (*lost, losed*) a game for the first time this season.

GO ON

9. The dark green trim *(made, maked)* a nice contrast with the fresh white paint.

10. We *(haved, had)* one more chance at success.

> **TIP** As you learn more irregular verbs, you will probably notice patterns in the way they make their past forms. For example, the verbs lend, send, and spend follow the same pattern. They each form their past and past participles by changing the last d to t. Learning these patterns may help you make verb forms correctly. Look for other patterns, too, as you study irregular verbs.

EXERCISE B Fill in the blank with the past or past participle form of the verb given in parentheses.

Examples 1. *(hear)* Mr. Devon ___*heard*___ that I am really good at math. [The correct past form

of the verb *hear* is *heard*.]

2. *(have)* He asked me if I had ___*had*___ fun in math class. [The correct past

participle form of the verb *have* is *had*.]

11. *(lose)* I told him I had never _________ a math contest. [What is the correct form of the past

participle of the verb *lose*?]

12. *(make)* I _________ good grades in math the last three years. [What is the correct past form of

the verb *make*?]

13. *(send)* Then Mr. Devon _________ me to the math tutorial lab.

14. *(have)* I have never _________ to go there before.

15. *(lend)* Mr. Devon said that he had _________ me to the math lab.

16. *(hear)* Then I _________ that I would be helping younger kids with their math.

17. *(spend)* Last week I _________ five hours helping kids with math homework.

18. *(make)* I know that I really _________ a difference for those kids when I was there!

19. *(lose)* Many of them have totally _________ their fears of math because of me.

20. *(have)* These kids have _________ fun with math problems and equations.

Irregular Verbs B

7c. An ***irregular verb*** forms its past and past participle in some other way than by adding *–d* or *–ed* to the base form.

Some irregular verbs make their past and past participle forms by changing vowels. Here are some common irregular verbs that change vowels in their past forms. Read these verbs aloud slowly. Become familiar with how they sound and how they look.

BASE FORM	PAST	PAST PARTICIPLE
become	became	[have] become
begin	began	[have] begun
come	came	[have] come
drink	drank	[have] drunk
hold	held	[have] held
lead	led	[have] led
ring	rang	[have] rung
run	ran	[have] run
shrink	shrank *or* shrunk	[have] shrunk
sing	sang	[have] sung
sink	sank *or* sunk	[have] sunk
swim	swam	[have] swum

EXERCISE A Underline the correct past or past participle form of the irregular verb in parentheses in each sentence. Remember to look for helping verbs such as *has, have,* and *had* if you are not sure which past form to use.

Examples 1. The weather *(becomed, became)* cold quite suddenly. [The correct past form of *become* is *became.*]

2. The chickadees have *(sang, sung)* their winter song cheerily. [The correct past participle form of *sing* is *sung.*]

1. Athletes from all over the district *(swum, swam)* the laps quickly and gracefully. [What is the correct past form of the verb *swim*?]

2. Has the package *(come, came)* in the mail yet? [What is the correct past participle form of the verb *come*?]

3. The doorbell *(rang, ringed)* just as Katie was setting her backpack down.

4. The deer *(ran, run)* across the hills.

5. Who *(lead, led)* the marching band out onto the field?

6. The rock Joseph threw *(sank, sinked)* to the bottom of the clear pond.

7. Every time I wash this sweater, it has *(shrinked, shrunk)* just a little more.

8. The rosebushes have *(held, holded)* onto their blooms until mid-October.

9. After the long race, the runners *(drunk, drank)* the cool water with relief.

10. When the play *(began, begun)*, the audience sat silently and listened.

> **TIP** As you learn more irregular verbs, you will probably notice patterns in the way they make their past forms. For example, the verbs *begin, drink, ring, shrink, sing, sink,* and *swim* follow the same pattern of vowel changes. The *i* in the base form *(begin, drink,* etc.) changes to an *a* in the past form *(began, drank,* etc.) and a *u* in the past participle form *(begun, drunk,* etc). Learning these patterns may help you make verb forms correctly. Look for other patterns, too, as you study irregular verbs.

EXERCISE B Fill in the blank with the past or past participle form of the verb given in parentheses. Remember to look for helping verbs such as *has, have,* and *had* if you are not sure which past form to use.

Examples 1. *(drink)* Has the cat ____*drunk*____ all its water? [The correct past participle form of the

verb *drink* is *drunk.*]

2. *(run)* The track team ____*ran*____ in a marathon last weekend. [The correct past

form of the verb *run* is *ran.*]

11. *(swim)* Mario has just _________ the length of a football field. [What is the correct form of the

past participle of the verb *swim*?]

12. *(lead)* The trail in the forest _________ directly to the campsite. [What is the correct past

form of the verb *lead*?]

13. *(sing)* Have you ever _________ in a choir?

14. *(come)* The detectives _________ upon an important clue.

15. *(begin)* The celebration _________ with a musical number.

16. *(hold)* Juanita _________ the baby carefully in her arms.

17. *(become)* The peaches on the tree slowly _________ ripe.

18. *(shrink)* Has my shirt _________ from the wash?

19. *(sink)* That building has _________ four inches in the last ten years.

20. *(run)* Have we _________ out of milk again?

Irregular Verbs C

| **7c.** | An ***irregular verb*** forms its past and past participle in some other way than by adding *–d* or *–ed* to the base form. |

Some irregular verbs make their past and past participle forms by changing vowels and consonants. Here are some common irregular verbs that change vowels and consonants in their past forms. Read these verbs aloud slowly. Become familiar with how they sound and how they look.

BASE FORM	PAST	PAST PARTICIPLE
buy	bought	[have] bought
do	did	[have] done
find	found	[have] found
freeze	froze	[have] frozen
get	got	[have] got *or* gotten
know	knew	[have] known
leave	left	[have] left
pay	paid	[have] paid
ride	rode	[have] ridden
teach	taught	[have] taught

TIP As you learn more irregular verbs, you will probably notice patterns in the way they make their past forms. For example, the verbs *blow, grow, know,* and *throw* follow the same pattern of consonant and vowel changes. Learning these patterns may help you make verb forms correctly. Look for other patterns, too, as you study irregular verbs.

EXERCISE A Underline the correct past or past participle form of the irregular verb in parentheses. Remember to look for helping verbs such as *has, have,* and *had* if you're not sure which past form to use.

Examples 1. Wendy's dad recently *(buyed, bought)* her a new bicycle helmet. [The correct past form of the verb *buy* is *bought*.]

2. Has the locker shelf *(broke, broken)* again? [The correct past participle form of the verb *break* is *broken*.]

1. Our dog has *(ridden, rode)* in our van many times. [What is the correct past participle form of the verb *ride*?]

2. We *(left, leaved)* without our house key again! [What is the correct past form of the verb *leave*?]

3. Has Ms. Sanchez *(sayed, said)* what we should read in our books tonight?

4. The child had *(drew, drawn)* a picture of flowers for her grandmother.

5. The ocean liner has *(gone, went)* halfway to Alaska by now.

6. The pond *(freezed, froze)* over last night.

7. Has the cat *(standed, stood)* at the top of the stairs all day?

8. The cafeteria staff had (*taken, tooken*) a much-deserved break.

9. Somebody has already (*ate, eaten*) all the leftover spaghetti!

10. How many journalists have (*written, wrote*) for that magazine?

A few irregular verbs make no change at all in their past and past participle forms. Here are some common irregular verbs that do not change at all in their past forms. Read these verbs aloud slowly. Become familiar with how they sound and how they look.

BASE FORM	PAST	PAST PARTICIPLE
burst	burst	[have] burst
cut	cut	[have] cut
hit	hit	[have] hit
put	put	[have] put
read	read	[have] read

EXERCISE B Fill in the blank with the past or past participle form of the verb given in parentheses. Remember to look for helping verbs such as *has, have,* and *had* if you are not sure which past form to use.

Examples 1. (*burst*) Alex nearly ___*burst*___ with excitement! [The past form of the verb *burst* is burst.]

2. (*lead*) Have you ever ___*led*___ the Pledge of Allegiance in your classroom? [The past participle form of the verb *lead* is *led*.]

11. (*cut*) Last February I _________ out Valentine's Day cards by hand. [What is the correct past form of the verb *cut*?]

12. (*sing*) The middle school folk group has recently _________ at a local music event. [What is the correct past participle form of the verb *sing*?]

13. (*read*) Our reading group has just _________ Louisa May Alcott's *Little Men*.

14. (*put*) Have you _________ away the dishes yet?

15. (*cut*) My father _________ the turkey at the dinner table.

16. (*burst*) Why hasn't that water balloon _________ yet?

17. (*hold*) The bookstore _________ this book for Gary until he could come and buy it.

18. (*hit*) The archer's arrow _________ the center of the target.

19. (*run*) The trains _________ on time on the opening day of the new light rail system.

20. (*drink*) The horses _________ deeply before they crossed the cool creek.

Introductory Course

Verb Tense

The Six Tenses

7d. The **tense** of a verb indicates the time of the action or the state of being that is expressed by the verb.

The time of an action can be past, present, or future. Each verb has six tenses. Each of the six tenses indicates a different way of expressing time.

Here are three tenses.

> **PRESENT** The band **marches.** [The present tense verb *marches* indicates an action that happens regularly.]
>
> **PRESENT PERFECT** The band **has marched.** [The present perfect tense verb *has marched* indicates an action that started to happen sometime before now. The action may continue into the present.]
>
> **PAST** The band **marched.** [The past tense verb *marched* indicates an action that happened in the past.]

EXERCISE A Identify the tense of the underlined verb in each of the following sentences. Write *present, present perfect,* or *past* on the line provided.

Example _____*present perfect*_____ **1.** Hasn't Liz <u>played</u> that song many times? [*Has played* is the

present perfect tense of the verb *play.*]

______________ **1.** Last Sunday the cruise ship <u>returned</u> to port. [The verb indicates an action

that happened last Sunday.]

______________ **2.** The lock on the door <u>latches</u> at the top.

______________ **3.** Has Marie <u>watched</u> that film yet?

______________ **4.** The bus always <u>stops</u> at railroad crossings.

______________ **5.** Yesterday we <u>planted</u> our cucumber seeds.

Here are three more tenses.

> **PAST PERFECT** The band **had marched.** [The past perfect verb *had marched* indicates an action that happened before a specific time in the past.]
>
> **FUTURE** The band **will march.** [The future tense verb *will march* indicates an action that will happen in the future.]
>
> **FUTURE PERFECT** The band **will have marched.** [The future perfect tense verb *will have marched* indicates an action that will have happened before a specific time in the future.]

GO ON

EXERCISE B Identify the tense of the underlined verb in each of the following sentences. Write *past perfect, future,* or *future perfect* on the line provided.

Example ___*future perfect*___ **1.** By the end of the week, we <u>will have studied</u> the first two

chapters. [*Will have studied* is the future perfect tense of *study.*]

_______________ **6.** The tomato plants <u>will wither</u> if we don't water them. [The verb indicates

an action that will happen in the future.]

_______________ **7.** Maureen wasn't sure whether she <u>had closed</u> the window.

_______________ **8.** Most of the stores <u>will open</u> early this Saturday.

_______________ **9.** By the time we get home, <u>will</u> Kate <u>have left</u> for school already?

_______________ **10.** Christine asked Tom whether he <u>had visited</u> the Grand Canyon.

The Progressive Form

Each of the six tenses also has a form called the *progressive form.* The progressive form expresses an action or state of being that keeps going on. The progressive form of a verb is made up of the appropriate form of *be* plus the verb's present participle.

REMINDER The present participle is the *–ing* form of the verb.

PRESENT PROGRESSIVE	The band **is marching.**
PAST PROGRESSIVE	The band **was marching.**
FUTURE PROGRESSIVE	The band **will be marching.**
PRESENT PERFECT PROGRESSIVE	The band **has been marching.**
PAST PERFECT PROGRESSIVE	The band **had been marching.**
FUTURE PERFECT PROGRESSIVE	The band **will have been marching.**

EXERCISE C Write the verb form indicated in parentheses on the line provided.

Example 1. Nina ___*will be auditioning*___ for the school play. (future progressive form of *audition*)

[*Will be auditioning* is the future progressive form of the verb *audition.*]

11. The nature festival _________________ a snake exhibit. (future tense of *feature*) [The future

tense is formed with *will.*]

12. Student council members _________________ donations for the food drive. (present

progressive tense of *collect*) [The present progressive includes the *–ing* form of the verb.]

13. When attacked, a porcupine _________________ its tail full of quills into the attacker.

(present tense of *drive*)

14. Michelle accidentally _________________ into the table. (past tense of *bump*)

15. Before today, I _________________ that museum only once. (past perfect tense of *visit*)

Sit and Set; Rise and Raise; Lie and Lay A

Sit and Set

The verb *sit* means "to be seated" or "to rest." *Sit* does not usually take a direct object. The verb *set* means "to put something in a place." *Set* usually takes a direct object.

> **EXAMPLES**   She **sat** on a pillow. [*Sat* means "to have been seated." There is no direct object.]
>
> **Did** you **set** that pillow on the bed? [*Did set* takes the object *pillow*.]

TIP▶ To choose between *sit* and *set*, try replacing the verb with a form of *put*. If the new sentence makes sense, then you will probably use a form of the verb *set*. If the new sentence does not make sense, then you will probably use a form of the verb *sit*.

> **EXAMPLES**   Earl *(set* or *sat)* the bowl on the counter. [Does *Earl put the bowl on the counter* make sense? Yes, so *set* is the right verb to use.]
>
> Lara and Ellen *(set* or *sat)* in front of us on the bus this morning. [Does *Lara and Ellen put in front of us on the bus this morning* make sense? No, so *sat* is the correct verb to use.]

EXERCISE A   Underline the correct verb in parentheses in each of the following sentences.

Example 1. Did you *(sit, set)* the flowerpot on the back porch? [*Set* means "to put something in a place." Its object is *flowerpot*.]

1. After dinner, we *(sat, set)* by the fire and talked. [Does the verb have an object?]

2. When we walked into the room, Dad was *(sitting, setting)* napkins on the table.

3. Did anyone *(sit, set)* in the bleachers?

4. The dog *(sat, set)* its rubber bone by the water dish.

5. Please don't *(sit, set)* your books on the couch.

Rise and Raise

The verb *rise* means "to go up" or "to get up." *Rise* does not take a direct object. The verb *raise* means "to lift something up" or "to cause something to rise." *Raise* usually takes a direct object.

> **EXAMPLES**   The kite **rose** high above the trees. [*Rose*, the past form of *rise*, means "went up" and does not take a direct object.]
>
> The wind **raised** the kite high above the trees. [*Raised*, the past form of *raise*, means "lifted" and takes the direct object *kite*.]

EXERCISE B   Underline the correct verb in parentheses in each of the following sentences.

Example 1. Dad *(rose, raised)* our allowance by fifty cents. [*Raised* means "caused to rise" and takes the direct object *allowance*.]

GO ON ➡

6. We woke up early, just as the sun was *(rising, raising)* over the lake. [Does the verb have an object?]

7. The eagle *(rose, raised)* high above the cliffs.

8. Please *(rise, raise)* the window.

9. The elevator *(rose, raised)* faster than we expected.

10. At the town meeting, residents *(rose, raised)* their hands when they had questions.

Lie and *Lay*

The verb *lie* usually means "to recline," "to be in a place," or "to remain lying down." *Lie* does not take a direct object. The verb *lay* usually means "to put something down" or "to place something." *Lay* usually takes a direct object.

> **EXAMPLES**   Susan **was lying** on the couch resting. [*Was lying* means "was reclining" and does not have an object.]
>
>   **Did** the builder **lay** the foundation for the house? [*Did lay* means "did place" and has the object *foundation*.]

TIP▶ As with the verb *set*, you can also substitute *put* for *lay*. If the sentence makes sense with *put*, use the appropriate form of *lay*. If the sentence does not make sense with *put*, use the appropriate form of *lie*.

> **EXAMPLES**   Anna is *(lying or laying)* the rug on the kitchen floor. [Does *Anna is putting the rug on the kitchen floor* make sense? Yes, so *laying* is the correct verb to use.]
>
>   Cindy will *(lie or lay)* down for a nap. [Does *Cindy will put down for a nap* make sense? No, so *lie* is the correct verb to use.]

EXERCISE C Underline the correct verb in parentheses in each of the following sentences.

Example 1. I will (<u>lie</u>, lay) on the sofa until I feel better. [*Lie* mean "recline" and does not take an object.]

11. The tomb of King Tutankhamen *(lay, laid)* undiscovered for hundreds of years. [Does the verb take an object?]

12. Did you *(lie, lay)* the place mats on the dining table?

13. The *Titanic* has *(lain, laid)* on the bottom of the ocean since it sank in 1912.

14. As Burt was leaving, he realized that he had *(lain, laid)* his keys on the seat of the car.

15. The Mississippi River *(lies, lays)* entirely in the United States.

Sit and *Set; Rise* and *Raise; Lie* and *Lay* B

Sit and *Set*

The verb *sit* means "to be seated" or "to rest." *Sit* does not usually take a direct object. The verb *set* means "to put something in a place." *Set* usually takes a direct object.

> **EXAMPLES** Carlton **sat** on the floor to read his magazine. [*Sat* means "to have been seated." There is no direct object.]
>
> **Has** Sandra **set** her purse on the table? [*Has set* takes the object *purse*.]

TIP To choose between *sit* and *set*, try replacing the verb with a form of *put*. If the new sentence makes sense, then you will probably use a form of the verb *set*. If the new sentence does not make sense, then you will probably use a form of the verb *sit*.

> **EXAMPLES** Please (*sit* or *set*) that plant near the window. [Does *Please put that plant near the window* make sense? Yes, so *set* is the right verb to use.]
>
> Are the twins (*sitting* or *setting*) together on the bus? [Does *Are the twins putting together on the bus?* make sense? No, so *sitting* is the correct verb to use.]

EXERCISE A Underline the correct verb in parentheses in each of the following sentences.

Example 1. Has Ken (*sit, set*) the glasses on the table? [*Set* means "to put something in a place." Its object is *glasses*.]

1. (*Sit, Set*) down and talk with us for a while. [Does the verb have an object?]

2. After sweeping the floor, Leo (*sit, set*) the broom inside the closet.

3. Please (*sit, set*) your books under your desk.

4. Mr. Gruber was (*sitting, setting*) next to Ms. Gruber at the restaurant.

5. Did Tracy (*sit, set*) in the front row?

Rise and *Raise*

The verb *rise* means "to go up" or "to get up." *Rise* does not take a direct object. The verb *raise* means "to lift something up" or "to cause something to rise." *Raise* usually takes a direct object.

> **EXAMPLES** Please **rise** when your name is called. [*Rise* means "get up" and does not take a direct object.]
>
> **Did** Bob **raise** his hand when he had a question? [*Did raise* means "did lift" and takes the direct object *hand*.]

EXERCISE B Underline the correct verb in parentheses in each of the following sentences.

Example 1. The tide (*raised, rose*) quickly. [*Rose* means "went up" and does not take a direct object.]

GO ON

6. Tyrone *(rose, raised)* the chair so that I could vacuum under it. [Does the verb have an object?]

7. Please *(raise, rise)* the window to let some fresh air inside.

8. After the bread *(rises, raises)*, the baker will put it in the oven.

9. Do you think Congress will *(rise, raise)* taxes next year?

10. Everyone in the courtroom *(rose, raised)* when the judge entered.

Lie and *Lay*

The verb *lie* usually means "to recline," "to be in a place," or "to remain lying down." *Lie* does not take a direct object. The verb *lay* usually means "to put something down" or "to place something." *Lay* usually takes a direct object.

> **EXAMPLES**   The hammer **was lying** on the workbench. [*Was lying* means "was in a place" and does not have an object.]
>
> The carpenter **laid** the hammer on the workbench. [*Laid* means "placed" and has the object *hammer.*]

TIP▶ As with the verb *set*, you can also substitute *put* for *lay*. If the sentence makes sense with *put*, use the appropriate form of *lay*. If the sentence does not make sense with *put*, use the appropriate form of *lie*.

> **EXAMPLES**   Nathan is *(laying* or *lying)* a welcome mat in front of the door. [Does *Nathan is putting a welcome mat in front of the door* make sense? Yes, so *laying* is the correct verb to use.]
>
> I usually *(lay* or *lie)* down to rest in the afternoon. [Does *I usually put down to rest in the afternoon* make sense? No, so *lie* is the correct verb to use.]

TIP▶ Notice that the past of *lie* and the base form of *lay* are the same: *lay*. Be careful not to confuse these two verbs.

> **EXAMPLES**   Please **lay** the files on my desk. [*Lay* is the present tense form of the verb *lay*. Please lay what? Files. *Files* is the direct object.]
>
> My scarf **lay** underneath my jacket. [*Lay* is the past tense form of the verb *lie*. There is no direct object.]

EXERCISE C   Underline the correct verb in parentheses in each of the following sentences.

Example 1. Jack *(lay, <u>laid</u>)* his socks next to the bed. [*Laid* mean "put" and takes the object *socks.*]

11. Tom was *(laying, lying)* in the hammock sleeping. [Does the verb take an object?]

12. The Hawaiian islands *(lay, lie)* in the Pacific Ocean.

13. The small baby *(laid, lay)* still in her crib.

14. Margo *(laid, lay)* a cover over the chair before painting the wall.

15. Did Yoko *(lie, lay)* the newspaper on the sofa?

The Forms of Personal Pronouns

Subject Form

A personal pronoun has different forms that show how the pronoun can be used in a sentence.

The *subject form* of a pronoun is used for subjects and predicate nominatives. Personal pronouns in the subject form include *I, you, he, she, it, you, we,* and *they.*

NOTE▶ The subject form of pronouns is also called the *nominative case.*

> **EXAMPLES** **He** and **I** take guitar lessons together. [*He* and *I* are subject pronouns.]
> Did **she** eat the last apple? [*She* is a subject pronoun.]

REMINDER▶ A *predicate nominative* usually follows a form of the verb *be* (such as *am, are, is, was, were, be, been,* or *being*) and identifies or refers to the subject of a sentence.

> **EXAMPLE** The youngest member of the swim team is **he.** [*He* is a predicate nominative that identifies the subject *member.*]

EXERCISE A Underline all of the subject pronouns in the following sentences.

Example 1. They are cousins. [*They* is a subject pronoun.]

1. We started a new project today. [What pronoun is the subject of the sentence?]

2. Do you have any pets?

3. The pitcher during the second inning was she.

4. Once I saw a bald eagle.

5. Are they coming to see the school play?

Object Form

The *object form* of a pronoun is used for direct objects, indirect objects, and objects of prepositions. Object pronouns include *me, you, him, her, it, us, you, them,* and *whom.*

> **EXAMPLES** Aunt Sophie invited **them** for a visit. [Whom did Aunt Sophie invite? *Them* is the direct object.]
> Thomas showed **us** his pet turtle. [To whom did Thomas show the turtle? *Us* is the indirect object.]
> **Whom** was the letter addressed to? [*Whom* is the object of the preposition *to.*]

NOTE▶ The object form is also called the *objective case.*

GO ON ▶

EXERCISE B   Underline the object form pronouns in the following sentences.

Example 1. Gerald saw <u>them</u> at the festival. [*Them* is an object pronoun.]

6. Jonathan gave me a calendar. [To whom did Jonathan give a calendar?]

7. Mario told her about the trip to Florida.

8. The Smiths always take the dog with them on vacation.

9. Was the delivery for us?

10. Claudia drew a picture of him.

Possessive Form

Possessive forms of pronouns are used to show ownership or possession. They include *my, mine, your, yours, his, her, hers, its, their, theirs, our,* and *ours.*

> **EXAMPLES**   Bees protect **their** hives. [The hives belong to the bees.]
> This notebook is **mine.** [The notebook belongs to me.]

NOTE▶ Unlike nouns, pronouns do not need an apostrophe when used to show possession.

> **INCORRECT**   That jacket is hers'.
> **CORRECT**   That jacket is **hers**.
> **INCORRECT**   Is that cat with the white paws yours' or theirs'?
> **CORRECT**   Is that cat with the white paws **yours** or **theirs**?

EXERCISE C   Read each of the following sentences. Then, think of a possessive pronoun that completes each sentence's meaning. Write the pronoun on the line provided. Hint: Some items have more than one correct answer.

Example 1. Charlie writes down all of _____*his*_____ class assignments in a school planner. [The pronoun *his* shows possession.]

11. I often misplace _______ house key. [Whose key was misplaced?]

12. Is this blue sweater _______?

13. Our dog Buck searched all over the house for _______ favorite toy.

14. Sarah keeps _______ sketches in a large folder.

15. The cast members looked wonderful in _______ costumes.

The Subject Form

Subjects

| **8a.** | Use the subject form of a pronoun that is the subject of a verb. |

The *subject* tells whom or what the sentence is about. Subject pronouns include *I, you, he, she, it, we, you, they,* and *who.*

EXAMPLES   **Who** brought the fruit salad? [*Who* is the subject of the verb *brought. Who* is a subject pronoun.]

Will **you** and **she** read the announcements next week? [*You* and *she* are the subjects of the verb *Will read.* Both pronouns are subject pronouns.]

I painted the picture, and **he** made the frame. [*I* is the subject of the verb *painted. He* is the subject of the verb *made.* Both pronouns are subject pronouns.]

TIP To choose the correct form of pronouns in compound subjects, try each pronoun by itself with the verb. Choose the pronouns that sound right with the verb.

ORIGINAL   *(Him, He)* and *(me, I)* went to a baseball game.

SEPARATE   *(Him, He)* went to a baseball game. *(Me, I)* went to a baseball game. [In the first sentence, *Him went* does not sound right. *He went* sounds right. In the second sentence, *Me went* does not sound right. *I went* sounds right.]

ANSWER   **He** and **I** went to a baseball game. [The correct pronouns are *He* and *I.*]

EXERCISE A   In each of the following sentences, underline the appropriate pronoun in parentheses.

Example 1. Do (*her, she*) and Anthony live in the same neighborhood? [The pronoun *she* is part of the complete subject, *she and Anthony. She* is a subject pronoun.]

1. The Maxwells and (*he, him*) rode into town together. [Which pronoun should be used as the subject of the verb *rode*?]

2. Neither (*her, she*) nor I went to the carnival.

3. Christopher and (*me, I*) always wear protective gear when skateboarding.

4. Will Michael and (*them, they*) repair the broken bicycle?

5. Do Jared and (*he, him*) know each other?

Predicate Nominatives

| **8b.** | Use the subject form for a pronoun that is a predicate nominative. |

A *predicate nominative* completes the meaning of a linking verb and refers to the subject of the sentence. A pronoun used as a predicate nominative usually follows a form of the verb *be,* such as *am, are, is, was, were, be, been,* or *being.*

GO ON

> **EXAMPLES**   My closest friend is **she.** [The pronoun *she* completes the meaning of the linking verb *is* and identifies the subject *friend*. *She* is a subject pronoun.]
> Were the only people there early **he** and **I?** [The pronouns *he* and *I* complete the meaning of the linking verb *were* and identify the subject *people*. Both pronouns are subject pronouns.]
>
> **TIP** To choose the correct form of a pronoun used as a predicate nominative, reverse the order of the words in the sentence so that the subject and the predicate nominative change places. Try each pronoun by itself with the verb. Choose the pronoun that sounds right with the verb.
>
> **ORIGINAL**   The man in the costume is (*he, him*).
> **REVERSED**   (*He, Him*) is the man in the costume. [*He is* sounds right. *Him is* does not sound right.]
> **ANSWER**   The man in the costume is **he.** [The correct pronoun is *he*.]

EXERCISE B   In each of the following sentences, underline the appropriate pronouns in parentheses.

Examples 1. Is the team captain (*she, her*)? [The pronoun *she* completes the meaning of the linking verb and identifies the *captain*.]

2. The candidates for the scholarship are (*he, him*) and she. [The pronouns *he* and *she* complete the meaning of the linking verb and identify the subject *candidates*.]

6. Were the sponsors of the event (*they, them*)? [Which pronoun is used as a predicate nominative to identify the *sponsors*?]

7. The swimmer with the fastest time is (*her, she*). [Which pronoun is used as a predicate nominative to identify the *swimmer*?]

8. The oldest member of the family is (*he, him*).

9. Will next year's officers be she and (*I, me*)?

10. Was that (*him, he*) who scored the winning run?

11. The first act in the talent show will be (*we, us*).

12. The woman in the back row is (*she, her*).

13. Near the front of the line were (*he, him*) and I.

14. Last year the secretary was (*him, he*).

15. Are the only ones who offered suggestions (*them, they*)?

for **CHAPTER 8: USING PRONOUNS CORRECTLY**   *pages 229–233*

The Object Form

Direct Objects

8c. Use the object form for a pronoun that is the direct object of a verb.

A *direct object* completes the meaning of an action verb. It tells *who* or *what* receives the action.

> **EXAMPLES**   Luis saw **her** at the mall. [Luis saw whom? *Her* is the direct object. It completes the meaning of the action verb *saw.*]
>
> **Whom** did you bring with you? [*Whom* is the direct object. It completes the meaning of the action verb *did bring.*]

REMINDER Object pronouns include *me, you, him, her, it, us, you, them,* and *whom.*

TIP To choose the correct pronoun when there is more than one object, try each pronoun by itself in the sentence. Choose the pronoun that sounds right.

> **EXAMPLE**   Vera followed Michael and (*I, me*) up the stairs.
>
> **SEPARATED**   Vera followed Michael up the stairs. Vera followed (*I, me*) up the stairs. [In the second sentence, *Vera followed I up the stairs* does not sound right. *Vera followed me up the stairs* does sound right.]
>
> **ANSWER**   Vera followed Michael and **me** up the stairs. [The correct pronoun is *me.*]

EXERCISE A Underline the appropriate form of pronouns in parentheses in each of the following sentences.

Example 1. All year long, that teacher supported him and (*we,* <u>*us*</u>). [The teacher supported whom? *Him* and *us* are the direct objects. They complete the meaning of the verb *supported.*]

1. The host greeted (*us, we*) at the door. [Whom did the host greet at the door?]

2. After I mowed the lawn, Mr. Jones paid (*I, me*).

3. Did you see (*her, she*) at the theater?

4. The gymnasts amazed her and (*he, him*) with their tumbling skills.

5. Mrs. Reed told (*they, them*) and us about the teams' performances.

Indirect Objects

8d. Use the object form for a pronoun that is the indirect object of a verb.

An *indirect object* tells *to whom* or *to what* or *for whom* or *for what* something is done. An indirect object may come between a direct object and an action verb.

> **EXAMPLES**   Patricia bought **me** a poster. [*Me* is the indirect object. *Me* tells *for whom* Patricia bought a poster. *Poster* is the direct object of the verb *bought.*]

GO ON

Mr. Garcia told **him** and **me** a story. [*Him* and *me* are the indirect objects. *Him* and *me* tell *to whom* Mr. Garcia told the story. *Story* is the direct object of the verb *told*.]

EXERCISE B In each of the following sentences, underline the appropriate form of pronouns in parentheses.

Example 1. The judges awarded (*he, him*) and her trophies. [*Him* and *her* are the indirect objects.

Him and *her* tell *to whom* the judges awarded trophies.]

6. My mother bought my sister and (*I, me*) matching outfits. [For whom were the outfits bought?]

7. Please send (*she, her*) your new address when you move.

8. Mario gave them and (*we, us*) invitations to his birthday party.

9. Danny won't tell (*he, him*) or me the answer to the riddle.

10. The police officer taught (*we, us*) a lesson about bicycle safety.

Objects of Prepositions

8e. Use the object form for a pronoun that is the object of a preposition.

A noun or a pronoun that follows a preposition is called the ***object of the preposition.***
Some examples of prepositions are *in, to, for, behind, around, above, with,* and *next to.*

EXAMPLE The Jacksons sat behind **us** at the game. [*Us* follows the preposition *behind. Us* is the object of the preposition *behind.*]

TIP▶ As with direct objects, when two or more pronouns follow a preposition, try each pronoun by itself to make sure that you have used the correct form. Choose the pronoun that sounds right.

EXERCISE C In each of the following sentences, underline the appropriate form of the pronouns in parentheses.

Example 1. The crow swooped above him and (*I, me*). [*Him* and *me* are objects of the

preposition *above.*]

11. After you finish the book, please give it to John or (*she, her*). [Which pronoun should be used as

the object of the preposition *to*?]

12. I hope the train doesn't leave without (*we, us*)!

13. Darlene divided the work between Sam and (*he, him*).

14. Nancy borrowed paper and pencils from (*he, him*) and her.

15. For (*who, whom*) are you making the birthday card?

Special Pronoun Problems

Pronouns with Appositives

Sometimes a pronoun is followed directly by a noun that identifies the pronoun. This noun is called an *appositive*.

> **EXAMPLE** We **friends** have similar hobbies. [*Friends* is the appositive identifying the pronoun *we*.]

TIP▶ To choose the correct pronoun before an appositive, delete the appositive and try each form of the pronoun separately. Choose the pronoun that sounds right.

> **EXAMPLE** The coach praised (*we, us*) athletes.
> **DELETED** The coach praised (*we, us*).
> **CORRECT** The coach praised (*we, us*) athletes.

EXERCISE A Underline the appropriate form of the pronoun in paretheses in each of the following sentences.

Example 1. (*We, Us*) girls are going to see a movie together. [The noun *girls* is the appositive identifying the subject *We.*]

1. (*We, Us*) tourists need help finding the museum. [Which sounds right—*We need* or *Us need*?]

2. Please bring (*we, us*) volunteers some water to drink.

3. I hope the announcer tells (*we, us*) fans why the game has been delayed.

4. Should (*we, us*) actors take our positions on stage?

5. (*We, Us*) newspaper reporters always check our sources.

Who and *Whom*

Like other pronouns, the pronoun *who* has a subject form and an object form. The subject form is *who*, and the object form is *whom*. Be careful to use the correct pronoun form in questions.

> **SUBJECT FORM** **Who** wrote this letter? [The pronoun is used as the subject of the verb *wrote*, so the pronoun is in the subject form.]
>
> **Who** will the next contestant be? [The pronoun is used as the predicate nominative of the verb *will be*, so the pronoun is in the subject form.]
>
> **OBJECT FORM** To **whom** was the letter delivered? [The pronoun is used as the object of the preposition *to*, so the pronoun is in the object form.]
>
> **Whom** did they select? [The pronoun is used as the direct object of the verb *did select*, so the pronoun is in the object form.]

GO ON ▶

EXERCISE B Circle the correct pronoun form in each of the following sentences.

Example 1. From *(who,* whom*)* did you hear that information? [The pronoun is used as the object

of the preposition *From,* so *whom* is the correct form.]

6. *(Who, Whom)* can I call to get the notes for the class I missed? [Is the prounoun used as the subject

or the direct object of the verb *can call*?]

7. *(Who, Whom)* will the new teacher be?

8. To *(who, whom)* should he give his research paper?

9. That trophy will go to the student *(who, whom)* wins the debate.

10. I gave the letter to Camille, for *(who, whom)* it was intended.

EXERCISE C Circle the correct pronoun form in each of the following sentences.

Examples 1. Sharon couldn't find *(we,* us*)* cheerleaders before the game. [The noun

cheerleaders is the appositive identifying the direct object *us.*]

2. *(Who,* Whom*)* won the chess tournament? [The pronoun is used as the subject of the

sentence, so *Who* is the correct form.]

11. *(Who, Whom)* did Charlotte ask? [Is the pronoun used as the subject of the sentence or as the

object of the verb?]

12. *(We, Us)* boys usually practice late on Thursdays.

13. The teacher sent *(us, we)* students to the library.

14. *(Who, Whom)* would like to walk the dog?

15. From *(who, whom)* did you get a ride to the game?

16. After practicing for two hours, *(we, us)* musicians were ready to perform.

17. *(Who, Whom)* called me yesterday?

18. My aunt asked *(we, us)* girls to cook dinner.

19. By lunchtime, *(we, us)* volleyball players had won two games.

20. To *(whom, who)* are you directing your question?

Forms of Modifiers

A *modifier* makes the meaning of a word or word group more specific. A modifier can be a word, a phrase, or a clause. The two kinds of modifiers are *adjectives* and *adverbs*.

One-Word Modifiers

9a.   *Adjectives* make the meanings of *nouns* and *pronouns* more specific.

>   **EXAMPLES**   The **blue** scarf is Adele's. [The adjective *blue* makes the meaning of *scarf* more specific. *Blue* tells *which* scarf.]
>
>   Is that jacket **new**? [The adjective *new* tells *what kind* of jacket.]

9b.   *Adverbs* make the meanings of verbs, adjectives, and other adverbs more specific.

>   **EXAMPLES**   The audience cheered **loudly.** [The adverb *loudly* makes the meaning of the verb *cheered* more specific. *Loudly* tells *how* the audience cheered.]
>
>   The engine was **extremely** hot. [The adverb *extremely* makes the meaning of the adjective *hot* more specific.]
>
>   Ally left **rather** suddenly. [The adverb *rather* makes the meaning of the adverb *suddenly* more specific.]

EXERCISE A   Tell whether the underlined word in each sentence is an adjective or an adverb. On the line provided, write *ADJ* for *adjective* or *ADV* for *adverb*.

Example   _ADV_   **1.** Derrick <u>often</u> plays basketball with his brother. [*Often* makes the meaning of the verb *plays* more specific.]

_______   **1.** The salad was made with <u>crisp</u> lettuce and fresh tomatoes. [Does *crisp* describe a noun, or does it tell more about a verb, an adjective, or an adverb?]

_______   **2.** <u>Soon</u> the leaves will change color.

_______   **3.** Please put the <u>dirty</u> dishes in the sink.

_______   **4.** Because of the fog, Blaine drove <u>slowly</u>.

_______   **5.** The weather will become <u>quite</u> cool next week.

Phrase and Clause Modifiers

Like one-word modifiers, phrases can also be used as adjectives and adverbs.

>   **EXAMPLES**   The house **with the iron fence** belongs to my cousin. [The phrase *with the iron fence* acts as an adjective that makes the meaning of *house* more specific. *With the iron fence* tells *which* house.]

GO ON

Chad found his lost sock **under the bed.** [The phrase *under the bed* acts as

an adverb and makes the meaning of the verb *found* more specific.

Under the bed tells *where* Chad found the sock.]

Clauses can also be used as modifiers.

REMINDER A clause is a word group that contains a subject and a verb.

EXAMPLES   **Once we finish our chores,** we can go to the park. [The clause *Once we*

finish our chores acts as an adverb that makes the meaning of the verb

can go more specific. *Once we finish our chores* tells *when* we can go.]

The group **that she likes best** will be in town next week. [The clause *that*

she likes best acts as an adjective that describes the noun *group. That she*

likes best tells *which* group.]

EXERCISE B Tell whether the underlined phrase or clause in each of the following sentences acts as an adjective or an adverb. On the line provided, write *ADJ* for *adjective* or *ADV* for *adverb*.

Examples   *ADJ*   **1.** The man with the whistle is Coach Harding. [The phrase describes the noun

man, so the phrase is an adjective.]

   ADV   **2.** We ate breakfast before we left for school. [The clause tells something about

the verb *ate,* so the clause is an adverb.]

______ **6.** The jet streaked across the cloudless sky. [Does the underlined phrase describe a noun, or

does it tell something about a verb, an adjective, or an adverb?]

______ **7.** The woman who spoke first is the chairperson. [Does the underlined clause describe a

noun, or does it tell something about a verb, an adjective, or an adverb?]

______ **8.** Jessica stashed her purse inside her locker. [Does the underlined phrase describe a noun

or tell something about a verb, an adjective, or an adverb?]

______ **9.** The roses in the green vase smell sweet.

______ **10.** The backpack with the red trim is mine.

______ **11.** Madagascar is the world's largest producer of vanilla.

______ **12.** Morning dew glistened on the leaves.

______ **13.** The quilt that is on my bed was my grandmother's.

______ **14.** Halley's comet was last visible from earth in 1986.

______ **15.** After Philip woke up, he went for a walk.

Degrees of Comparison

9c. The three degrees of comparison of modifiers are the *positive,* the *comparative,* and the *superlative.*

(1) The *positive degree* is used when only one thing is being described and no comparison is being made.

> **EXAMPLE** This room is **messy.** [*Messy* is a positive degree adjective. *Messy* describes only one thing—*room.*]

(2) The *comparative degree* is used when two things are being compared.

> **EXAMPLE** The cheetah ran **faster** than the lion. [*Faster* is a comparative degree adverb. *Faster* compares how two animals, the cheetah and the lion, ran.]

(3) The *superlative degree* is used when three or more things are being compared.

> **EXAMPLE** Monday is the **busiest** day of the week. [*Busiest* is a superlative degree adjective. *Busiest* compares *Monday* to all the other days of the week.]

EXERCISE A In each of the following sentences, identify the degree of the underlined modifier. On the line provided, write *positive, comparative,* or *superlative.*

Example _comparative_ **1.** These shoes are more comfortable than those. [The modifier compares two things, one pair of shoes to another pair of shoes.]

_______________ **1.** Founded in 1636, Harvard is the oldest university in the United States. [Does the modifier compare two things or more than two things?]

_______________ **2.** Water dripped noisily from the leaky faucet.

_______________ **3.** Are mittens warmer than gloves?

_______________ **4.** I can see more clearly with my glasses than without them.

_______________ **5.** Of the three Egyptian pyramids at Giza, the Great Pyramid is the largest.

Most one-syllable modifiers form the comparative degree by adding –*er* and the superlative degree by adding –*est.*

	POSITIVE	COMPARATIVE	SUPERLATIVE
ONE-SYLLABLE MODIFIER	near	near**er**	near**est**

Most two-syllable modifiers form the comparative degree by adding –*er* or by using *more.* They form the superlative degree by adding –*est* or by using *most.*

	POSITIVE	COMPARATIVE	SUPERLATIVE
TWO-SYLLABLE MODIFIERS	easy	easi**er**	easi**est**
	hopeful	**more** hopeful	**most** hopeful

GO ON ➡

NOTE Some two-syllable modifiers can form comparisons either way.

	POSITIVE	COMPARATIVE	SUPERLATIVE
EXAMPLE	friendly	friendl**ier**	friendl**iest**
	friendly	**more** friendly	**most** friendly

Modifiers that have three or more syllables form the comparative degree by using *more* and the superlative degree by using *most*.

	POSITIVE	COMPARATIVE	SUPERLATIVE
THREE-SYLLABLE MODIFIER	sensible	**more** sensible	**most** sensible

All modifiers form the decreasing comparative degree by using *less*. They form the decreasing superlative degree by using *least*.

	POSITIVE	COMPARATIVE	SUPERLATIVE
DECREASING COMPARISON	loyal	**less** loyal	**least** loyal

EXERCISE B On the lines provided, write the comparative and superlative degrees of the modifiers given.

Example 1. young _______*younger*_______ _______*youngest*_______

[*Young* has one syllable, so the comparative is formed by adding *–er,* and the superlative is formed by adding *–est.*]

Positive	Comparative	Superlative
6. colorful		

[How can the comparative and superlative forms of a three-syllable modifier be formed?]

Positive	Comparative	Superlative
7. sensitive		
8. gently		
9. brave		
10. often		
11. weak		
12. thoughtful		
13. creatively		
14. witty		
15. awkwardly		

Regular and Irregular Comparison

Regular Comparison

Most modifiers that have only one syllable form the comparative degree by adding *–er* and the superlative degree by adding *–est*.

	POSITIVE	COMPARATIVE	SUPERLATIVE
ONE-SYLLABLE MODIFIER	small	small**er**	small**est**

REMINDER The *comparative degree* is used when two things or groups of things are being compared. The *superlative degree* is used when three or more things or groups of things are being compared.

Modifiers that have two syllables form the comparative degree by adding *–er* or by using *more*.

	POSITIVE	COMPARATIVE	SUPERLATIVE
TWO-SYLLABLE MODIFIER	early	earli**er**	earli**est**

Modifiers that have three or more syllables form the comparative degree by using *more* and the superlative degree by using *most*.

	POSITIVE	COMPARATIVE	SUPERLATIVE
MULTI-SYLLABLE MODIFIER	energetic	**more** energetic	**most** energetic

To show **decreasing comparison,** use *less* to form the comparative degree and *least* to form the superlative degree.

DECREASING COMPARATIVE Backgammon is **less popular** with my friends than checkers.

DECREASING SUPERLATIVE My **least favorite** game is volleyball.

EXERCISE A Complete each of the following sentences with the appropriate comparative or superlative form of the adjective or adverb given in italics. Note: Some items ask you to fill the blank with a decreasing comparison.

Example 1. *funny (decreasing comparison)* Of all the comedians, the last one was the

_____least funny_____. [The modifier is comparing more than two things, so the superlative

form is used. The decreasing superlative is formed by adding *least*.]

1. *loudly*   That last thunderclap crashed _____________ than the one before. [Does the modifier

compare two things or more than two?]

2. *lively*   Highly social animals, chimpanzees are _____________ than gorillas.

3. *capably*   Delia plays the _____________ of all the violinists in the orchestra.

4. *sturdy (decreasing comparison)*   The _____________ chair in the room is the one in the corner.

5. *rapidly*   Human beings can run _____________ than snakes can move.

GO ON

Irregular Comparison

The comparative and superlative degrees of some modifiers are irregular in form.

The rules for forming irregular comparisons do not match those for forming regular comparisons. For example, most irregular comparatives and superlatives do not end in *–er* and *–est*.

POSITIVE	COMPARATIVE	SUPERLATIVE
good	better	best
well	better	best
bad	worse	worst
many	more	most
much	more	most

COMPARATIVE   That science fiction novel was **worse** than the mystery I read last month. [*Worse* is the comparative degree of *bad*.]

SUPERLATIVE   That science fiction novel was the **worst** book I have ever read. [*Worst* is the superlative degree of *bad*.]

EXERCISE B Complete each of the following sentences with the appropriate comparative or superlative form of the adjective or adverb given in italics.

Examples 1. *much* I have ___*more*___ free time in the morning than in the afternoon. [The modifier compares two things, so the comparative form is used.]

2. *good* This is the ___*best*___ film I have ever seen. [The modifier compares more than two things, so the superlative form is used.]

6. *bad* The weather seems __________ today than it did yesterday. [Does the modifier compare two things or more than two things?]

7. *many* __________ people vacation in Florida than in Ohio. [Does the modifier compare two things or more than two things?]

8. *well* Caleb feels __________ this week than he did last week.

9. *good* This guitar produces a __________ sound than that one.

10. *much* Elaine spends __________ time reading than Andrea does.

11. *bad* The team with the __________ record in the league won the championship.

12. *much* Of everyone in the family, Blake has the __________ patience.

13. *many* Denise bought __________ apples than bananas.

14. *good* John Milton is often considered one of the __________ poets of the English language.

15. *well* Of all her classes, Jana likes math __________.

Introductory Course

Special Problems in Using Modifiers

Double Comparisons

9f. Avoid using double comparisons.

Comparative modifiers are formed in one of two ways: (1) by adding *–er* or *–est* or (2) by adding *more* or *most*. When you make a comparison, you should use only one of these forms, not both. A ***double comparison*** occurs when a person mistakenly puts these two forms together.

> **NONSTANDARD**   We ate at the most newest restaurant in town. [*Most newest* uses both *most* and the *–est* ending to make a single comparison. *Most newest* is a double comparison.]
>
> **STANDARD**   We ate at the **newest** restaurant in town.

> **REMINDER▶** Irregular comparisons do not use *–er/–est*, *more/most*, or *less/least*. Adding these endings to an irregular modifier makes a double comparison. Some irregular modifiers are *better*, *best*, *worse*, *worst*, *more*, and *most*.

> **NONSTANDARD**   The team played worser this week than last week. [*Worser* is a double comparison. *Worse* by itself is used to make a single comparison between two things or groups of things.]
>
> **STANDARD**   The team played **worse** this week than last week.

EXERCISE A Each of the following sentences contains a double comparison. Circle the double comparison, and then write the appropriate form of the comparison on the line provided.

Examples 1. Emily is the student with the ~~mostest~~ friends. __*most*__ [*Most* is already superlative. Adding *–est* makes it a double comparison.]

2. Founded in the sixteenth century, Saint Augustine, Florida, is the ~~most oldest~~ city in the United States. __*oldest*__ [*Oldest* is already superlative. Adding *most* makes it a double comparison.]

1. My headache feels worser this afternoon than this morning. __________ [Which modifier is forming the comparative in two ways?]

2. Which trees in the park are the most tallest? __________ [Which modifier is forming the superlative in two ways?]

3. The movie ended more sooner than I expected. __________

4. Venus is the most brightest planet in the nighttime sky. __________

5. Who gave Mrs. Wilkins her most favoritest book? __________

6. The ostrich can grow more larger than the emu. __________

7. I like spinach more better than I like broccoli. __________

GO ON ▶

8. The damage to the car is worser than I thought. __________

9. Did Melissa write the bestest essay on trees? __________

10. Our lawn is more greener than our neighbor's lawn. __________

Double Negatives

9g.   Avoid using double negatives.

People use negative words all the time in everyday speaking and writing. You should not use
two or more negative words together to express one negative idea. If you do this, you create a
double negative. Some examples of negative words are *barely, hardly, neither, never, no, nobody,
none, no one, not (n't), nothing, nowhere,* and *scarcely*.

> **NONSTANDARD**   I don't have hardly any pencils left. [*Not (n't)* and *hardly* are both negative
> words. You should not use them together to express one negative idea.]
>
> **STANDARD**   I have hardly any pencils left.

EXERCISE B Each of the following sentences contains a double negative. Revise each sentence to
eliminate the double negative.

Examples 1. In class, no one never speaks out of turn. [Both *no one* and *never* are negative.]
    In class, no one ever speaks out of turn.

2. I can't barely hear what you are saying. [Both *n't* and *barely* are negative.]
    I can barely hear what you are saying.

11. Don't leave no wet clothes on the floor. [Which two words are negative?]

____

12. Hardly nobody showed up for the rally. [Which two words are negative?]

____

13. We won't never forget Mr. Major's kindness.

____

14. The Sanchezes hadn't scarcely finished dinner when the doorbell rang.

____

15. Even though the show was over, no one went nowhere.

____

Placement of Modifiers

9h. Place modifying words, phrases, and clauses as close as possible to the words they modify.

Where you place a modifier affects the meaning of a sentence.

> **EXAMPLES** Arlene said she would go to the library **before noon.** [In this sentence, *before noon* seems to modify *go.* The modifier tells when Arlene will go to the library.]
>
> **Before noon,** Arlene said she would go to the library. [In this sentence, *Before noon* is closer to the verb *said.* The modifier tells when Arlene made the statement.]

Sometimes, people accidentally change the meaning of a sentence by putting a modifier in the wrong place. A *misplaced modifier* seems to describe a word that the writer or speaker didn't mean for it to describe. If you remember to put modifiers close to the words they describe, you'll communicate more clearly.

> **EXAMPLES** She **only** watches ice skating. [She watches ice skating, but she doesn't skate herself.]
>
> She watches **only** ice skating. [She watches nothing but ice skating.]

EXERCISE A Draw an arrow from each misplaced modifier to its appropriate place in each of the following sentences. Hint: All misplaced modifers have been underlined for you.

Example 1. I read a book that was written by Nathaniel Hawthorne last week. [*Last week* seems to tell when Nathaniel Hawthorne wrote the book. It needs to be closer to the word it modifies, *read.*]

1. Van Gogh nearly painted *Sunflowers* 150 years ago. [*Nearly* seems to be modifying *painted.* Where should it go to modify *150 years ago*?]

2. We watched a film that was directed by Ron Howard today.

3. Some sunflowers almost grow up to fifteen feet high.

4. Josh and I visited some ruins left by ancient American Indians last week.

5. Overhead, we watched as the balloon sailed into the sky.

Prepositional Phrases A *prepositional phrase* includes a preposition, an object of the preposition, and any modifiers of that object. The *object of the preposition* is a noun or a pronoun.

Prepositional phrases can be used as adjectives and as adverbs.

REMINDER An *adjective* modifies a noun or a pronoun. An *adverb* modifies a verb, an adjective, or another adverb.

When a prepositional phrase is used as an adjective, it is usually placed directly after the word it modifies.

MISPLACED   I placed a box on the table of tissue. [Is the table filled with tissues? The prepositional phrase *of tissue* seems to modify *table*, but the sentence doesn't make sense this way. *Of tissue* acts as an adjective and should be placed closer to the noun *box*.]

CLEAR   I placed a box **of tissue** on the table. [*Of tissue* acts as an adjective and belongs after the word it modifies, *box*.]

A prepositional phrase used as an adverb should be placed near the word it modifies.

MISPLACED   Bruce will tour a building designed by Thomas Jefferson in May. [Did Thomas Jefferson design the building in May? *In May* acts as an adverb that tells when Bruce will tour. *In May* should be placed closer to the verb *will tour*.]

CLEAR   **In May,** Bruce will tour a building designed by Thomas Jefferson. [*In May* acts as an adverb and belongs near the verb *will tour*.]

Adjective Clauses   An *adjective clause* modifies a noun or a pronoun. Most adjective clauses begin with words such as *that, which, who, whom,* or *whose.* You should place adjective clauses directly after the word or words they modify.

MISPLACED   The band members met with the director who needed extra practice. [Did the director need extra practice?]

CLEAR   The band members **who needed extra practice** met with the director. [The clause *who needed extra practice* belongs directly after *band members*.]

EXERCISE B   Draw an arrow from the misplaced prepositional phrase or adjective clause in each of the following sentences to its appropriate location in the sentence. Hint: Misplaced phrases and clauses have been underlined for you.

Example   1.   My Aunt Edna sent me a birthday present, who lives in Chicago. [The adjective clause must be closer to the noun it modifies, *Aunt Edna*.]

6.   Mrs. Palmer lives down the street who drives a convertible. [What noun does the adjective clause modify?]

7.   Leslie said during lunch she would try out for the school play.

8.   Some pennies were made during World War II of steel.

9.   The fish is swimming in the bowl with a gold tail.

10.   Delores sends greeting cards to her friends that she makes herself.

Glossary of Usage A

accept, except *Accept* is a verb that means "to receive." *Except* may be used as a verb or as a preposition. Used as a verb, *except* means "to excuse" or "to leave out." Used as a preposition, *except* means "excluding" or "but."

> **EXAMPLES** David **accepted** advice from his guitar instructor. [You can replace *accept* with *received*.]
>
> The injured players were **excepted** from practice. [You can replace *excepted* with *excused*.]
>
> Everyone **except** Charles enjoyed the tour of the museum. [You can replace *except* with *but*.]

TIP To help you remember the difference between *accept* and *except*, try thinking of the *x* in *except* as an X-ing out, or canceling, of something.

ain't Do not use the nonstandard word *ain't* in formal situations.

> **NONSTANDARD** There **ain't** enough books for everyone.
>
> **STANDARD** There **aren't** enough books for everyone.
>
> **NONSTANDARD** He **ain't** marching in the parade.
>
> **STANDARD** He **isn't** marching in the parade.

anyways, anywheres, everywheres, nowheres, somewheres These words should not end in *s*.

> **EXAMPLE** The matching red sock is **somewhere** [not *somewheres*] in my room.

EXERCISE A In each of the following sentences, underline the word in parentheses that is correct according to formal, standard English.

Examples 1. Will the test cover all of the chapters *(accept, except)* the first one? [You can replace *except* with *but*.]

2. I looked *(everywhere, everywheres)* for the lost library book. [The word *everywhere* should not end in an *s*.]

1. On Tuesdays, senior citizens are *(accepted, excepted)* from paying full price. [Which word means "excused"?]

2. Isn't there a gas station *(somewhere, somewheres)* near here? [Should the word end in an *s*?]

3. Please *(accept, except)* my apology.

4. *(Ain't, Isn't)* he taking his camera with him to the zoo?

5. I was *(accepted, excepted)* from taking the test, but I have to make it up by next week.

6. You *(ain't, aren't)* leaving yet, are you?

7. Everyone received a letter today *(accept, except)* Roger.

8. We searched *(everywheres, everywhere)* for the missing house key.

9. Did you *(accept, except)* Clara's invitation?

10. Daniel brought everything for the party *(accept, except)* the drinks.

---

bad, badly   *Bad* is an adjective; it modifies nouns and pronouns. *Badly* is an adverb; it modifies verbs, adjectives, and adverbs.

EXAMPLES   Playing with my dog always cheers me up when I've had a **bad** day. [The adjective *bad* modifies the noun *day.*]

The rotten eggs smelled **bad.** [The adjective *bad* modifies the noun *eggs.*]

After it was injured, the dog limped **badly.** [The adverb *badly* modifies the verb *limped.*]

between, among   Use *between* when you are referring to two individuals or things at a time. Use *among* when you are referring to a group rather than to separate individuals or items.

EXAMPLES   Jeanine sat **between** Linda and Rebecca. [*Between Linda and Rebecca* refers to two people.]

The debate team discussed the topic **among** themselves. [*Among themselves* refers to a group of individuals.]

EXERCISE B   In each of the following sentences, underline the word in parentheses that is correct according to formal, standard English.

Examples 1. Please keep the secret *(between, among)* you and me. [*Between you and me* refers to two people.]

2. He felt *(badly, bad)* about missing his sister's piano recital. [The adjective bad modifies *he.*]

11. Last summer, I had a *(bad, badly)* fall at camp and broke my leg. [Which word would you use to modify the noun *fall*?]

12. The rabbit ran *(between, among)* the fence and the barn. [Which word would you use to refer to two things?]

13. Did the children behave *(bad, badly)* in front of the guests?

14. The band director passed out music *(between, among)* the band members.

15. She felt *(bad, badly)* about what she had said.

16. Are there any bad apples *(between, among)* the good ones?

17. Our team played *(bad, badly)* during the first half of the game.

18. Raul parked the car *(between, among)* the station wagon and the van.

19. Cigarettes are *(bad, badly)* for your health.

20. When will the teacher divide the lab assignments *(between, among)* the students?

for **CHAPTER 10: A GLOSSARY OF USAGE**   *pages 271–275*

Glossary of Usage B

could of   Do not use *of* with the helping verb *could*. Instead, write *could have*. Also avoid *ought to of, should of, would of, might of,* and *must of.*

> **EXAMPLE**   Gloria **could have** [not *could of*] spent more time studying.

fewer, less   Use *fewer* with plural words. Use *less* with singular words. *Fewer* tells "how many"; *less* tells "how much."

> **EXAMPLES**   This parking lot holds **fewer** cars than the parking lot across the street. [*Cars* is plural, so *fewer* is used.]
>
> There is **less** daylight in the winter than in the summer. [*Daylight* is singular, so *less* is used.]

TIP Use *fewer* with things you can count. Use *less* with things you cannot count.

EXERCISE A In each of the following sentences, underline the word or word group in parentheses that is correct according to formal, standard English.

Examples 1. I (*must of, must have*) left my wallet at home. [*Have* is used with the helping verb *must.*]

       2. There are (*fewer, less*) fish in the large tank than in the small one. [*Fish* is plural, so *fewer* is used.]

1. Does New York have (*fewer, less*) airports than California? [Which word should you use with a plural word?]

2. Matt (*could of, could have*) read for hours. [What verb should you use with the helping verb *could*?]

3. There is (*fewer, less*) rust on this shovel than on that one.

4. I (*should of, should have*) done my homework earlier.

5. Are (*fewer, less*) students entering the science fair this year?

6. A liter bottle holds (*fewer, less*) liquid than a gallon jug.

7. Someone (*might of, might have*) left a message on my answering machine.

8. There is (*fewer, less*) soap in this dispenser than in that one.

9. We (*ought to of, ought to have*) been more careful.

10. My recipe for vegetable soup calls for (*fewer, less*) ingredients than my mother's.

GO ON

learn, teach   *Learn* means "to gain knowledge." *Teach* means "to instruct" or "to show how."

> **EXAMPLES**   Our French club is **learning** about customs in the Provence region of France.
> [The club is gaining knowledge.]
>
> Mr. Richard is also **teaching** us about French history. [Mr. Richard is
> instructing.]

suppose to, supposed to   Do not leave off the *d* at the end of *supposed* when you write
supposed to.

> **EXAMPLE**   We are **supposed to** [not *suppose to*] meet them for dinner.

than, then   *Than* is used in making comparisons. *Then* means "next" or "after that."

> **EXAMPLES**   My new bicycle is larger **than** my old one. [*Than* is used to compare the
> new bicycle with the old one.]
>
> Luke turned out the lights, and **then** he went to bed. [*Then* indicates that
> Luke went to bed after he turned out the lights.]

TIP To help you remember the difference between *than* and *then*, think of the phrase *then is
when. Then* refers to time.

EXERCISE B In each of the following sentences, underline the word or word group in parentheses that is
correct according to formal, standard English.

Examples 1. My grandmother (*learned, taught*) me how to quilt. [Grandmother was instructing, so

taught is correct.]

2. We packed our suitcases and (*than, then*) loaded them into the car. [*Then* indicates

that the suitcases were loaded into the car after they were packed.]

11. Fresh fruit is usually tastier (*than, then*) canned fruit. [Which word is used to make comparisons?]

12. Will you (*learn, teach*) us about the weather? [Which word means "to instruct"?]

13. We put the jigsaw puzzle together and (*than, then*) took it apart again.

14. The speaker is (*suppose to, supposed to*) give a presentation on the formation of the Grand Canyon.

15. Mrs. Vega (*learned, taught*) her children how to play the violin.

16. The winner was announced, and (*than, then*) everyone applauded.

17. Am I (*suppose to, supposed to*) bring my own supplies?

18. We are (*teaching, learning*) about Africa in our social studies class.

19. Does Bianca pitch the softball faster than (*than, then*) Samantha?

20. Jupiter is farther from the sun (*than, then*) Mercury is.

First Words; Letter Salutations and Closings; The Pronoun *I*

First Words

11a. Capitalize the first word in every sentence.

> **EXAMPLES**   **T**he dog ran to the house. [*The* is the first word of the sentence.]
>
> **W**ho wants some popcorn? [*Who* is the first word of the sentence.]

EXERCISE A   Circle the letter that should be capitalized in each of the following sentences.

Example 1. (w)hat is your name? [The *w* in *what* should be capitalized because it is the first word of

the sentence.]

1. have you ever seen a mummy? [Is the first word of the sentence capitalized?]

2. the mummies in this museum are from Egypt.

3. some mummies have been found in Peru.

4. many objects were buried with the mummies.

5. sometimes robbers broke into the burial places.

Quotations

When a writer repeats someone else's exact words, the writer needs to put quotation marks at the beginning and end of the other person's words. Whenever you quote a sentence, begin the quoted sentence with a capital letter. You should do this even when the quoted sentence begins in the middle of a longer sentence.

> **EXAMPLES**   Kim shouted, "**T**hat car is going too fast!" [*That* is capitalized because it is the first word of the sentence that is quoted.]
>
> "**T**hat car is going too fast!" shouted Kim. [*That* is the first word of the sentence that is quoted. *That* is also the first word of the longer sentence.]

EXERCISE B   Circle the letter that should be capitalized in each of the following sentences.

Example 1. Sam said, "(t)he movie starts at seven o'clock." [The *t* in *the* should be capitalized

because *the* is the first word in a quoted sentence.]

6. "can your father give us a ride?" asked Sam. [Is the first word of the quoted sentence capitalized?]

7. Susanna said, "yes, I think he can."

8. "my brother can pick us up after the movie," said Sam.

9. "does he have his own car?" asked Susanna.

10. Sam said, "no, he drives my parents' car." 

Developmental Language Skills

Letter Salutations and Closings

11b. Capitalize the first word in both the salutation and the closing of a letter.

SALUTATIONS **D**ear Dr. Smith:	**D**earest Grandmother,
CLOSINGS **S**incerely yours,	**L**ove,

NOTE▶ Except for names and titles, the first word is the only word that is capitalized in a salutation or closing.

EXERCISE C Circle the letter that should be capitalized in each salutation or closing below.

Example 1. Ⓥery truly yours, [The *v* in *very* should be capitalized because it is the first word of the closing of a letter.]

11. my dear Aunt Mary, [Is the first letter of this salutation capitalized?]

12. yours truly,

13. dear Mom and Dad,

14. sincerely,

15. dear Mr. Jacobs:

The Pronoun *I*

11c. Capitalize the pronoun *I*.

In English, the word *I* is always capitalized. Capitalize *I* even if it is not the first word of a sentence. Also capitalize *I* whenever you use it in a contraction, such as *I've* or *I'd*.

EXAMPLES Maria and **I** are cousins.

Did you know that **I**'ve been a guitarist for three years?

EXERCISE D Circle the letter that should be capitalized in each of the following sentences.

Example 1. Ⓘ'm going to the library now. [The word *I* should always be capitalized, even in a contraction.]

16. Let's see if i've got two dollars. [Is the word *I* capitalized?]

17. Do you think i can ride with you?

18. What time do i have to be home?

19. He forgot that i'd already walked the dog.

20. May i sit here, please?

Proper Nouns A

11d. Capitalize proper nouns.

A *proper noun* is the name of a particular person, place, thing, or idea. Proper nouns are capitalized. A **common noun** is the name of a type of person, place, thing, or idea. A common noun generally is not capitalized unless it begins a sentence or is part of a title.

COMMON NOUNS	**p**oet	**c**ity	**m**onth
PROPER NOUNS	**R**obert **F**rost	**O**maha	**S**eptember

NOTE▶ Some proper nouns have more than one word. Capitalize all the important words.

EXAMPLES **P**eter the **G**reat   *Pride and Prejudice*   **B**ay of **B**iscay

EXERCISE A Circle the correctly capitalized word group in each of the following pairs.

Example 1. (Abraham Lincoln)   George washington

[Both first and last names should be capitalized, so Abraham Lincoln is the correctly

capitalized word group in this pair.]

1. north carolina   West Virginia

[Which word group is a proper noun that is capitalized correctly?]

2. California   State

3. his dog Pooch   the Dog that was lost

4. ella fitzgerald   Anita Simpson

5. a Month ago   in August

Names of People and Animals

Capitalize the names of people and animals. When a name has initials, capitalize the initials.

EXAMPLES **F**ranklin **D. R**oosevelt   my cat **T**iger   **E. B. W**hite

EXERCISE B Circle each letter that should be capitalized in the following sentences.

Example 1. I am reading some poems by emily dickinson. [*Emily Dickinson* should be capitalized

because these words name a specific person.]

6. My father's name is lawrence b. johnson. [Which words are parts of a person's name?]

7. Are rita and anna at school today?

8. Here is a biography of florence nightingale.

9. I think you will enjoy e. l. konigsburg's books.

10. The name of our new puppy is goldie.   **GO ON** ➡

Developmental Language Skills   **97**

Titles of People

11h.   Capitalize titles.

Always capitalize the title of a person when the title comes before the person's name, even if the title is abbreviated. Titles that do not come before names usually are not capitalized.

> **EXAMPLE**   **Dr.** Nelda Fellows has been a **d**octor for thirty years. [The title *Dr.*, which is the abbreviation for *Doctor,* comes before the person's name and should be capitalized. The word *doctor* does not come before a person's name.]

EXERCISE C   Circle each letter that should be capitalized in the following sentences. Draw a slash through each letter that is capitalized but should be lowercase.

Example 1.   Does that car belong to m̶rs. Simpson? [*Mrs.* comes before the name *Simpson.*]

11. He is a well-known Professor. [Which word is a title that does not come before a person's name?]

12. Our guest speaker today is major Katherine Gibbs.

13. Have you met mr. and mrs. Gonzales?

14. I have an appointment with the Doctor this afternoon.

15. Her report is about president Carter.

A word that shows a family relationship is capitalized when the word comes before the person's name or is used in place of the person's name.

> **EXAMPLE**   Ask **M**om if we can go. [*Mom* is used instead of a person's name.]

Do not capitalize a word showing a family relationship when a possessive pronoun comes before the word.

> **EXAMPLE**   Have you met my **a**unt Christina? [The word *aunt* follows the possessive pronoun *my.*]

EXERCISE D   Circle each letter that should be capitalized in the following sentences. Draw a slash through each letter that is capitalized but should be lowercase.

Example 1.   Help g̶randma set the table, please. [*Grandma* is used in place of the person's name.]

16. You should send your Aunt Emily a birthday card. [Which word shows a family relationship? Does the word follow a possessive?]

17. I am helping dad paint the fence.

18. My Cousins Joe and Kevin have new bicycles.

19. Your father and grandpa Jefferson are in the backyard.

20. Did uncle Raymond call this afternoon?

for **CHAPTER 11: CAPITAL LETTERS**   *pages 288–290*

Proper Nouns B

Geographical Names

11d. Capitalize proper nouns.

Geographical names are proper nouns and should be capitalized. Geographical names include places such as countries, states, street names, and natural landmarks.

> **EXAMPLES** **S**outh **A**merica [continent]   **F**rance [country]
> **M**ontana [state]   **C**hicago [city]
> **P**acific **O**cean [body of water]   **C**entral **A**venue [street]
> **M**ount **L**ogan [mountain]   **E**verglades **N**ational **P**ark [park]

NOTE When words like *north, south, western,* or *northeastern* are used in the name of a region, they are proper nouns and should be capitalized. When you use these words to show a direction, do not capitalize them.

> **EXAMPLES** My grandparents are from the **S**outh. [region]
> Drive **n**orth on the highway for ten miles. [directions]

EXERCISE A Circle each letter that should be capitalized in the following sentences.

Examples 1. Have you ever been to **f**lorida? [The word *Florida* names a particular place and should

      be capitalized.]

    2. The store is on the north side of **w**ellington **a**venue. [The words *Wellington Avenue*

      name a specific place and should be capitalized. The word *north* is lowercase because it is

      used here as a direction, not a region.]

1. Frank has lived in brazil and costa rica. [Which words name specific places?]

2. Does the mississippi river flow through missouri? [Which words name particular places or natural landmarks?]

3. The river empties into the gulf of mexico near new orleans.

4. Many people have climbed mount everest.

5. My family saw the bats at carlsbad caverns national park.

6. The ancient city of athens is still the capital of greece.

7. In 1927, Charles Lindbergh made the first solo flight across the atlantic ocean.

8. When you come to the first stoplight, turn west onto broad street.

9. The world's largest desert is on the continent of africa.

10. The capital city of california is sacramento.

Organizations

The names of organizations, teams, and institutions are proper nouns and should be capitalized.

> **EXAMPLES**   **A**merican **L**ibrary **A**ssociation [organization]
>
> **G**olden **V**alley **H**igh **S**chool Hornets [team]
>
> **G**eorge **W**ashington **U**niversity **M**edical **C**enter [institution]

EXERCISE B Circle each letter that should be capitalized in the following sentences.

Example 1. We went to a meeting of the african-american family history association. [All parts of the name of a specific organization should be capitalized.]

11. This publication is from the american heart association. [Which words name an organization?]

12. The bears and the hornets are playing at the stadium today.

13. My sister has applied to georgetown university.

14. We went on a field trip to the los angeles county museum of art.

15. The river city high school rockets are in the playoffs this year.

The names of government bodies are proper nouns and should be capitalized.

> **EXAMPLES**   **C**ongress of the **U**nited **S**tates [government body]
>
> **F**ederal **C**ommunications **C**ommission [government agency]

NOTE▶ Abbreviations of the names of organizations, institutions, and government bodies are often a set of capital letters.

> **EXAMPLES**   **N**ational **A**eronautics and **S**pace **A**dministration   **NASA**
>
> **O**rganization of **A**merican **S**tates   **OAS**

EXERCISE C Circle each letter that should be capitalized in the following sentences.

Example 1. The plans were approved by the environmental protection agency (epa). [Environmental Protection Agency names a specific government agency and should be capitalized. All letters in the abbreviation for the agency should be capitalized.]

16. Each state elects two members of the u.s. senate. [Which words name a specific governmental body?]

17. She works for the fbi in Washington, D.C.

18. The madison city council will meet tomorrow afternoon.

19. This bank is insured by the fdic (federal deposit insurance corporation).

20. We will visit the headquarters of the united nations in New York.

Proper Nouns C

Dates and Events

11d. Capitalize proper nouns.

The names of the days of the week, the months of the year, and holidays are proper nouns and are capitalized. The names of the seasons of the year are not usually capitalized.

EXAMPLES	**T**hursday [day of the week]	**M**ay [month of the year]
	Memorial **D**ay [holiday]	**s**ummer, **w**inter [seasons]

Be sure to capitalize the names of important events and periods in history. The names of other kinds of special events are also capitalized.

EXAMPLES	**C**ivil **W**ar [historical event]
	Bronze **A**ge [historical period]
	Carr **C**ounty **F**air [special event]

EXERCISE A Circle each letter that should be capitalized in the following sentences.

Example 1. Those men and women are veterans of the Vietnam War. [*Vietnam War* names a

specific historical event and should be capitalized.]

1. Let's volunteer to help with the special olympics. [Which words name a special event?]

2. On presidents' day we honor the birthdays of George Washington and Abraham Lincoln.

3. Joe has practice after school on wednesday.

4. My family always goes to the beach in july.

5. The dark ages followed the collapse of the Roman Empire.

Nationalities and Religions

The names of nationalities, races, and peoples are proper nouns and are capitalized. You should also capitalize the names of religions, religious holy days, celebrations, and sacred writings.

EXAMPLES	**C**anadian [nationality]	**H**mong [people]
	Islam [religion]	**P**alm **S**unday [holy day]
	Torah [sacred writings]	

EXERCISE B Circle each letter that should be capitalized in the following sentences.

Example 1. Devout followers of Islam pray five times a day. [*Islam* is the name of a specific

religion and should be capitalized.]

6. A major religion in India is hinduism. [Which word names a specific religion?]

7. Does your family celebrate christmas?

GO ON

8. Her great-grandparents are italian.

9. The maya built an amazing civilization in southern Mexico and Central America.

10. The jewish celebration of passover takes place in March or April each year.

Vehicles and Buildings

Ships, trains, aircraft, and spacecraft often have specific names. They should be capitalized.

EXAMPLES   the *Niña* [ship]   the *Spirit of St. Louis* [airplane]

The names of specific buildings, monuments, and other structures are capitalized. Do not capitalize the name of a type of building unless the word is part of the building's name.

EXAMPLES   Jefferson Memorial [monument]   Sydney Opera House [building]

EXERCISE C Circle each letter that should be capitalized in the following sentences.

Example 1. The view from the top of the washington monument is great! [*Washington Monument* is the name of a specific monument and should be capitalized.]

11. The white house is at 1600 Pennsylvania Avenue. [Which words name a specific building?]

12. Shuttle flights were stopped for several years after the explosion of the *challenger* in 1986.

13. Everyone has heard about the sinking of the *titanic*.

14. Abraham Lincoln was shot while he was watching a performance at ford's theatre.

15. The statue of liberty was a gift to the United States from France.

Space

The names of planets, stars, constellations, and other heavenly bodies should be capitalized.

EXAMPLES   Neptune [planet]   Spica [star]
              Cassiopeia [constellation]   Milky Way [galaxy]

EXERCISE D Circle each letter that should be capitalized in the following sentences.

Example 1. I can usually find the constellation orion. [*Orion* is the name of a specific constellation and should be capitalized.]

16. The smallest planets are mercury and pluto. [Which words are the names of specific planets?]

17. The bright stars pollux and castor are in the constellation gemini.

18. The nearest spiral galaxy to our own is andromeda.

19. The first recorded sightings of halley's comet were made about 240 B.C.

20. Can you find the group of stars called the big dipper?

Titles of Creative Works

11h. Capitalize titles.

Whenever you write the title of a book, magazine, painting, movie, or other creative work, be sure to capitalize the first word, the last word, and all other important words in the title. Capitalize these words in subtitles, too. Don't capitalize articles (*a, an,* or *the*), conjunctions (such as *and* or *but*), or short prepositions (such as *of, into, by,* or *with*), unless the word is the first or last word in the title or subtitle.

The titles of some creative works are also written in italic letters or are underlined.

EXAMPLES	*Ender's Game* [book]	*It's a Wonderful Life* [movie]
	Popular Science [magazine]	*Nighthawks* [painting]
	USA Today [newspaper]	*The Thinker* [sculpture]
	Our Town [play]	*The Firebird* [long musical work]

EXERCISE A Circle each letter that should be capitalized in the following sentences.

Examples 1. My favorite book is *to kill a mockingbird*. [Except for the article *a*, all the words in this

title should be capitalized.]

2. My little sister reads *hop on pop* at least twice a day. [The word *on* is a short preposition

and should not be capitalized.]

1. Last weekend we watched the movie *north by northwest*. [Which words in the title are important

words?]

2. The orchestra played *tales from the vienna woods*, by Johann Strauss. [Which words in the title are

prepositions or articles?]

3. This is a photograph of *bronco buster*, a sculpture by Frederic Remington.

4. I found an article about bicycles in *outdoor life*.

5. Reporters from the *arkansas democrat-gazette* covered the story.

6. Arthur Miller's play *death of a salesman* won a Pulitzer prize.

7. The class has been reading Hemingway's *the old man and the sea*.

8. This painting is called *early sunday morning*.

9. My sister found the recipe in an old issue of *good housekeeping*.

10. Charles Dickens' book *a christmas carol* has been made into a movie many times.

GO ON ▶

for **CHAPTER 11: CAPITAL LETTERS**   **pages 299–302**   *continued*

The titles of shorter creative works follow the same rules of capitalization. The titles of shorter creative works are enclosed in quotation marks. Do not underline or italicize these titles.

> **EXAMPLES**   "**T**rees" [poem]
>
> "**T**he **R**ansom of **R**ed **C**hief" [short story]
>
> "**P**eople of the **R**eindeer" [article in a magazine]
>
> "**S**ilent **N**ight" [song]

EXERCISE B Circle each letter that should be capitalized in the following sentences.

Examples 1. The choir sang "(a)merica the (b)eautiful." [*America* and *Beautiful* should be capitalized.

The article *the* should not be capitalized because it is not the first or last word of the title.]

2. According to "(w)hy (d)ogs (c)hase (c)ats," dogs just want to be friends with cats again.

[All of the words in this title are important, so they should be capitalized.]

11. Almost everyone has finished reading O. Henry's story "the gift of the magi." [Which words in

the title are important? Which word is an article that is also the first word of the title?]

12. "stopping by woods on a snowy evening" is a well-known poem by Robert Frost. [Which

words in the title are important?]

13. My favorite Robert McCloskey story about Homer Price is "mystery yarn."

14. The audience joined in when we sang "this land is your land."

15. We have read "the raven" and "annabel lee," two poems by Edgar Allan Poe.

16. In less than six seconds, Sean can recite "the duck."

17. My article, "teachers talk television," will be in this week's paper!

18. Our principal said we looked sleepy, so she sang "i'm a little teapot."

19. She started rock collecting after she read "volcanoes and gemstones!"

20. Let's talk about the story "what do fish have to do with anything?"

Commas

Commas with Items in a Series

12f.   Use commas to separate items in a series.

A *series* is three or more items written one after the other. The items in the series may be either single words or word groups.

> **EXAMPLES**   The corn was **fresh, sweet, juicy,** and **delicious.** [This series has four single words. Commas separate these four words.]
>
> We **planted the corn, tended it, cooked it,** and **ate it.** [This series has four word groups. Commas separate these four word groups.]

NOTE ▶ When all the items in a series are joined by *and*, *or*, or *nor*, do not use commas to separate the items.

> **EXAMPLE**   Did she run **or** walk **or** jog? [The three items in this series are all joined by *or*. No commas are necessary.]

EXERCISE A In the following sentences, add commas where they are needed to separate items in a series.

Example 1.   I wash my hands before I eat, after I play with my dog, and before I go to bed.

      [*Before I eat, after I play with my dog,* and *before I go to bed* are word groups in a series.

      Commas separate the three word groups.]

1. I read three chapters turned out the light and fell asleep. [Which word groups are in a series?]

2. Do you want a green red or purple gel pen?

3. Julia plays soccer runs track and takes piano lessons during the school year.

4. Your jacket must be in the car in the house or at school.

5. When I have a test when I have a difficult assignment or when I'm having trouble with one of my subjects, my dad helps me study.

Commas with Adjectives

12g.   Use commas to separate two or more adjectives that come before a noun.

> **EXAMPLE**   One last spike ended the **fast, exciting** game. [The adjectives *fast* and *exciting* come before the noun *game*. These two adjectives are separated by a comma.]

REMINDER ▶ A *noun* is a word or word group that is used to name a person, a place, a thing, or an idea. An *adjective* is a word that is used to modify a noun or a pronoun.

GO ON ▶

Sometimes the last adjective in a series is thought of as part of the noun. In that case, do not use a comma before the last adjective.

> **EXAMPLE**   One last spike ended the **fast, exciting volleyball** game. [The adjective *volleyball* is thought of as part of the noun *volleyball game,* so there is no comma between *exciting* and *volleyball*.]

TIP To see whether a comma is needed between two adjectives, insert *and* between the adjectives. If *and* sounds awkward there, do not use a comma.

> **EXAMPLE**   One last spike ended the fast exciting volleyball game.
>
> **TEST**   One last spike ended the fast **and** exciting **and** volleyball game. [Place a comma wherever adding *and* makes sense. The *and* between *fast* and *exciting* makes sense. The *and* between *exciting* and *volleyball* sounds awkward.]
>
> **FINAL SENTENCE**   One last spike ended the **fast, exciting** volleyball game. [Add a comma between *fast* and *exciting* to replace the *and* in your test.]

Another test you can use is to switch the order of the adjectives. If the sentence still makes sense when you switch the adjectives, use a comma.

> **EXAMPLE**   One last spike ended the fast exciting volleyball game.
>
> **TESTS**   One last spike ended the **exciting fast** volleyball game. [The sentence still makes sense when *fast* and *exciting* have been switched.]
>
> One last spike ended the exciting **volleyball fast** game. [The sentence does not make sense when *fast* and *volleyball* have been switched.]
>
> **FINAL SENTENCE**   One last spike ended the **fast, exciting** volleyball game. [Add a comma between *fast* and *exciting,* since these two adjectives can be switched.]

EXERCISE B   In the following sentences, add commas where they are needed to separate two or more adjectives that come before a noun.

Example   1. At the thrift store I found a pair of sturdy**,** affordable in-line skates. [The adjective *in-line* is thought of as part of the noun *in-line skates.* The two adjectives *sturdy* and *affordable* come before the noun *in-line skates* and should be separated by commas.]

6. Did you like the short lively tune the band just played? [Which two adjectives should be separated by a comma?]

7. The clean shiny chrome sparkled in the sunlight.

8. The small brown furry squirrel jumped from tree to tree.

9. What an intelligent thoughtful speech he gave!

10. His wild spiked hair wouldn't stay inside the baseball cap.

Commas and Semicolons with Compound Sentences

Commas with Compound Sentences

12h. Use a comma before *and, but, for, nor, or, so,* or *yet* when it joins independent clauses in a compound sentence.

REMINDER An *independent clause* is a word group that can stand alone as a complete sentence and has a subject and a verb. A *compound sentence* is a sentence that contains two or more independent clauses.

EXAMPLES Will you go to the store**, or** should I go instead? [The two independent clauses *Will you go to the store* and *should I go instead* are joined by a comma and the word *or.*]

We hurried home**, yet** we were still late for dinner. [The two independent clauses *We hurried home* and *we were still late for dinner* are joined by a comma and the word *yet.*]

EXERCISE A In the following sentences, add commas where they are needed before an *and, but, for, nor, or, so,* or *yet* that joins two or more independent clauses.

Examples 1. They haven't called us**,** nor have they written to us about the trip. [*Nor* joins the two independent clauses *They haven't called us* and *have they written to us about the trip.*]

2. We could sweep the floor**,** or we could vacuum it. [*Or* joins the two independent clauses *We could sweep the floor* and *we could vacuum it.*]

1. We wanted to walk all the way but we forgot our sneakers. [Which word joins two independent clauses?]

2. Felicia shot the last basket and she won the game for our team! [Which word joins two independent clauses?]

3. Terence is my best friend but I don't always agree with him.

4. The boys played well in the semifinals yet they did not win the championship.

5. I ironed my shirt but it got wrinkled in the suitcase.

6. Did you want to ride with us to the soccer game or did you want to meet us there?

7. I developed the pictures but I didn't bring them with me.

8. The script wasn't well written nor were the characters well developed.

9. I wanted to do well on the test so I went to the review session after school.

10. Have you read the book or did you see the movie?

GO ON

12m. Use a semicolon between parts of a compound sentence if they are not joined by *and, but, for, nor, or, so,* or *yet.*

    EXAMPLES We're due at home in ten minutes; we need to hurry! [The independent clauses *We're due at home in ten minutes* and *we need to hurry* are not joined by *and, but, for, nor, or, so,* or *yet,* so they are joined by a semicolon.]

NOTE▶ Independent clauses should be joined by a semicolon only if the ideas in the independent clauses are closely related. If the clauses are not closely related, then use a period to make two separate sentences.

    SEMICOLON I studied very hard all morning; I got an A on the test. [The two ideas are closely related, so the two independent clauses *I studied very hard* and *I got an A on the test* are joined by a semicolon.]

    PERIOD I studied very hard all morning. For breakfast I had oatmeal. [The ideas are not closely related, so a period is used to make the two independent clauses *I studied very hard* and *For breakfast I had oatmeal* two separate sentences.]

EXERCISE B In the following sentences, add commas and semicolons where they are needed.

Examples 1. Most of my friends love soccer; I love football. [The two independent clauses *Most of my friends love soccer* and *I love football* are not joined by *and, but, for, nor, or, so,* or *yet.* They should be joined with a semicolon.]

    2. Samantha lost her gloves, and I helped her find them. [The two independent clauses *Samantha lost her gloves* and *I helped her find them* are joined by *and.* A comma is needed before *and.*]

11. My dad made me a bookshelf I helped him. [Are the two independent clauses joined by *and, but, for, nor, or, so,* or *yet?*]

12. Amy was on her skateboard Luisa was on her bicycle. [Are the two independent clauses joined by *and, but, for, nor, or, so,* or *yet?*]

13. I would come with you but I should walk my dog right now.

14. Kim ate all of her lunch I couldn't finish all of mine.

15. The bells rang at 1:23 everyone looked startled.

16. I wrote a letter to the editor and my older sister checked my spelling and punctuation.

17. Dad's computer was making a strange noise I thought it was broken.

18. There are eighteen windows in the house eleven of them are downstairs.

19. We signed up for the race our goal is to place in the top twenty.

20. My grandmother always cheers me up but I don't see her often enough.

for CHAPTER 12: PUNCTUATION   **page 327**

Colons

12n. Use a colon before a list of items, especially after expressions such as *the following* and *as follows.*

> **EXAMPLES** My sewing kit contains **the following** items: needles, thread, scissors, and buttons.
>
> Which additional item will you need for the experiment: a small ruler, a magnifying glass, or a book of matches?

NOTE ▸ Do not use a colon between a preposition and its objects or between a verb and its objects.

> **INCORRECT** My sewing kit contains: needles, thread, scissors, and buttons. [The colon comes between the verb, *contains*, and its objects, *needles, thread, scissors,* and *buttons.*]
>
> **CORRECT** My sewing kit contains needles, thread, scissors, and buttons.
>
> **INCORRECT** Please send the packages to: the lobby, the office, and the gatehouse. [The colon comes between the preposition *to* and its objects *lobby, office,* and *gatehouse.*]
>
> **CORRECT** Please send the packages to the lobby, the office, and the gatehouse.

EXERCISE A In the following sentences, place colons where they are needed. If a sentence is correct, write *C* on the line provided.

Examples _______ 1. These foods make up my favorite meal: baked chicken, broccoli, and salad. [The sentence contains a list of items, *baked chicken, broccoli,* and *salad,* and it needs a colon before the list.]

_____*C*_____ 2. The tools you will need are a hammer, a chisel, and a saw. [In this sentence, the verb *will need* is followed by a list, *a hammer, a chisel, and a saw.* Since a colon must not go between a verb and its objects, the sentence does not need a colon and is correct.]

_______ **1.** Have the following people turned in their assignments Greg, Brenda, Isabel, and Carlton? [Where does the list of items begin?]

_______ **2.** The varieties of trees we planted are as follows live oak, crape myrtle, and elm. [Where does the list of items begin?]

_______ **3.** You will need the following items on your first day at school pencils, a ruler, notebook paper, an eraser, and a ballpoint pen.

_______ **4.** Your story should have a theme, a conflict, plot development, a climax, and a resolution.

_______ **5.** The student council is holding elections for the following positions president, vice-president, secretary, and treasurer.

GO ON ▸

_______ **6.** There are three things you should remember speak clearly, speak slowly, and tell the truth.

_______ **7.** I brought souvenirs for my mother, my father, my sister, and my best friend.

_______ **8.** There are three places you should start looking for clues for the scavenger hunt the basement, the linen closet, and the attic.

_______ **9.** Can you bring me the following cleaning products furniture polish, tile cleaner, scouring powder, and carpet deodorizer?

_______ **10.** A dictionary entry contains the word, its pronunciation, its part of speech, its etymology, and its definition.

12o.	Use a colon between the hour and the minute when you write the time.

   EXAMPLES 3**:**30 P.M.   10**:**45 in the morning

12p.	Use a colon after the salutation of a business letter.

   EXAMPLES Dear Chief Inspector Friedman**:** Dear Mrs. Fowler**:**

EXERCISE B In the following items, add colons where they are needed.

 Examples 1. School will be dismissed early today at 2**:**15. [A colon separates the hour and the minute.]

    2. Dear Superintendent Dawson**:** [A colon is used after the salutation of a business letter.]

11. She has to be at volleyball practice at 5 15 this afternoon. [What does the colon separate when you write the time?]

12. Dear Mr. Wells [What follows the salutation of a business letter?]

13. Please set your alarm for 7 15 A.M., so you can be at school by 8 30.

14. Dear Officer Scott

15. Did you say that band practice starts at 1 00 this afternoon?

16. Does the orchestra begin playing at 6 30 or 7 00?

17. Dear Sir or Madam

18. Dear Mayor Garcia

19. The bus will leave at 8 15 in the morning.

20. Dear Dr. Moore

Underlining (Italics) and Quotation Marks with Titles

Underlining Titles

13a. Use underlining (italics) for titles and subtitles of books, plays, periodicals, films, television series, works of art, and long musical works.

When you write the title of a book, a play, a movie, a magazine, a newspaper, or some other major creative work, underline the entire title. A typesetter would set underlined words in *italics*, letters that lean to the right. If you use a computer, you can probably set these titles in italics yourself. Do not underline titles that you have set in italics. Use underlining or italics, but not both.

ITALICIZED	UNDERLINED	
Foundation and Empire	<u>Foundation and Empire</u>	[book]
Architectural Digest	<u>Architectural Digest</u>	[magazine]
Newsday	<u>Newsday</u>	[newspaper]
The Skin of Our Teeth	<u>The Skin of Our Teeth</u>	[play]
Lawrence of Arabia	<u>Lawrence of Arabia</u>	[movie]
Nova	<u>Nova</u>	[television series]
The Night Watch	<u>The Night Watch</u>	[work of art]
The Marriage of Figaro	<u>The Marriage of Figaro</u>	[long musical work]

REMINDER Capitalize the first word, the last word, and all important words in the titles of creative works such as books, movies, short stories, poems, and works of art.

EXERCISE A Underline any title that should be in italics in each of the following sentences. Be sure to underline every word of the title.

Examples 1. The drama students are performing <u>Alice in Wonderland</u>. [*Alice in Wonderland* is

underlined because it is the title of a play.]

2. We're going to discuss an article from <u>The Riverside Daily News</u>. [*The Riverside Daily News* is underlined because it is the title of a newspaper.]

1. We watched the movie West Side Story in class last week. [What is the title of the movie?]

2. This painting by Magritte is called The Human Condition. [Is *The* this title's first word?]

3. Have you ever read Robinson Crusoe?

4. The photographs in National Geographic are really beautiful.

5. Did you see the editorial in today's Morning Advocate?

6. My parents grew up watching a show called Wild Kingdom.

7. Mozart's comic opera The Magic Flute is funny!

8. Who titled this sculpture The Seated Sakyamuni?

9. President Kennedy's book Profiles in Courage won a Pulitzer Prize.

10. Which character in the movie Toy Story is bravest?

Quotation Marks with Titles

13l. Use quotation marks to enclose the titles of short works such as short stories, poems, newspaper or magazine articles, songs, episodes of television series, and chapters and other parts of books.

The titles of short stories, poems, and songs are enclosed in double quotation marks. You should also use quotation marks around the titles of newspaper or magazine articles, chapters of books, and episodes of television series. Do not underline or use italics for these titles.

> **EXAMPLES**   "Old Ironsides" [poem]
>
>   "The Purloined Letter" [short story]
>
>   "West End Blues" [song]
>
>   "Super Potatoes" [article in a magazine]

EXERCISE B Place quotation marks wherever they are needed in the sentences below.

Example 1. Cecil has memorized most of "The Charge of the Light Brigade." ["The Charge of the Light Brigade" is in quotation marks because it is the title of a poem.]

11. Washington Irving wrote the story The Legend of Sleepy Hollow. [Do quotation marks enclose this title?]

12. My little brother sang Jingle Bells for two hours last night!

13. Jenny can recite the poem The Dragons are Singing Tonight by Jack Prelutzky.

14. Can you play the song Greensleeves on the recorder?

15. The article called How to Clean Your Room in Five Minutes is very funny.

EXERCISE C Write a title for each kind of creative work below. Use underlining or quotation marks where they are needed. You can make up a title if you don't know one.

Example 1. Movie   *The Maltese Falcon*   [*The Maltese Falcon* is underlined because it is the title of a movie.]

16. song   [Are song titles underlined, or are they enclosed in quotation marks?]

17. book   ________________

18. poem   ________________

19. painting ________________

20. play   ________________

Quotation Marks

13c. Use quotation marks to enclose a ***direct quotation***—a person's exact words.

Be sure to place quotation marks before and after a person's exact words.

> **EXAMPLE**   John said, "I will be home after school." [Quotation marks surround John's exact words. John is the speaker.]

When you tell a story, you sometimes explain what somebody said, rather than repeat the person's exact words. When you reword what another person has said, you are using an indirect quotation. Do not use quotation marks for an ***indirect quotation***—a rewording of a direct quotation.

> **EXAMPLE**   John said that he would be home after school. [The sentence rewords what John said. John did not say the words *he would be home after school*, so no quotation marks surround these words.]

EXERCISE A   Insert quotation marks around the speaker's exact words in the following sentences.

Examples 1. Dan said, "Lunch looks good today." [Dan's exact words were *Lunch looks good today.* There are quotation marks at the beginning and at the end of these words.]

      2. "Let's go to the store," said Ted. [Ted's exact words were *Let's go to the store.* There are quotation marks at the beginning and at the end of these words.]

1. When did the bell ring? asked Nick. [What were Nick's exact words?]

2. David said, I have to be home at six o'clock. [What were David's exact words?]

3. Max shouted, Look at those elephants!

4. I finished all my homework, said Ann.

5. Uncle Phil stopped the car and said, Do you need a ride?

6. Is the door locked? asked Angela.

7. We can go to my house after school, said Rita.

8. You remembered my birthday! exclaimed Simon.

9. Sara asked, What time is the party?

10. I will pick you up at seven o'clock, said Dad.

GO ON

A sentence that is a direct quotation begins with a capital letter. You should begin a quoted sentence with a capital letter even when the quoted sentence begins in the middle of a longer sentence.

> **EXAMPLE**   Mary shouted, "**H**ere comes the parade!" [The *H* in *Here* is capitalized because it is the first letter of the quoted sentence.]

Sometimes a person's exact words are interrupted by an explanation of who is talking. If a quoted sentence continues after the interruption, the second part of the quotation begins with a lowercase letter. If the second part of the quotation is a complete sentence, the first letter should be capitalized.

> **UNDIVIDED**   "She doesn't know the answer, but she can look it up," said Ray. [Ray's exact words are one sentence. One set of quotation marks surrounds Ray's exact words.]
>
>   "I like cats. We have three," said Sharon. [Sharon's exact words are two sentences. One set of quotation marks surrounds Sharon's exact words.]
>
> **DIVIDED**   "She doesn't know the answer," said Ray, "but she can look it up." [Quotation marks surround each part of Ray's exact words. The *b* in *but* is lowercase because the second part of the quotation is part of the quoted sentence.]
>
>   "I like cats," said Sharon. "We have three." [Quotation marks surround each part of Sharon's words. The *W* in *We* is capitalized because the second part of the quotation is a complete sentence.]

EXERCISE B   Circle each letter that should be capitalized in these sentences. Draw a slash through each letter that is capitalized but should be lowercase.

Example 1. "ⓓid you borrow my bike," asked Jim, "/Or does Larry have it?" [The *D* in *Did* is capitalized because *Did* is the first word of the quoted sentence. The *o* in *or* is lowercase because the second part of the quotation is not a complete sentence.]

11. "I will help you with those problems," said Frank, "If you remember to bring your book."

     [Is the second part of the quotation a complete sentence?]

12. "this problem is really hard," said Kristin, "but I'll get it right this time."

13. "When," asked Miguel, "Are the science projects due?"

14. Evan pointed and said, "my project is on that table."

15. "if you are hungry," said Nancy, "you can make a sandwich."

Apostrophes A

Possessive Nouns

The *possessive case* of a noun is the form of the noun that shows ownership. This form is made by adding an apostrophe and often an *s* to the noun. Be careful where you place apostrophes, or you may confuse your reader.

13m. To form the possessive case of a singular noun, add an apostrophe and an *s*.

> **EXAMPLE** the child**'s** toys [The toys belong to one child. The apostrophe comes after the singular noun *child* and before the *s*. The *s* in this example shows possession and does not make the noun *child* plural.]

13n. To form the possessive case of a plural noun that does not end in *s*, add an apostrophe and an *s*.

> **EXAMPLE** the children**'s** toys [The toys belong to more than one child. The plural noun *children* does not end in *s*, so the apostrophe comes before the *s*.]

13o. To form the possessive case of a plural noun ending in *s*, add only the apostrophe.

> **EXAMPLE** the bicycles**'** wheels [The wheels belong to more than one bicycle. The noun *bicycles* is the plural form of *bicycle*, so the apostrophe follows the *s*.]

EXERCISE A Write the possessive form of each of the following words. Write your answers on the lines provided.

Example 1. cats _____*cats'*_____ [The word *cats* is plural and ends in *s*. The possessive form is made by adding an apostrophe.]

1. men __________ [Is the word *men* plural? Does it end in *s*?]

2. mother __________

3. fox __________

4. window __________

5. babies __________

Possessive Pronouns

13p. Do not use an apostrophe with possessive personal pronouns.

Possessive Personal Pronouns

Common possessive pronouns are *my, mine, your, yours, our, ours, her, hers, his, its, their,* and *theirs.*

GO ON ➡

13q. To form the possessive case of many indefinite pronouns, add an apostrophe and an *s*.

Common Possessive Indefinite Pronouns

anyone's	either's	everyone's	neither's
nobody's	no one's	one's	somebody's

EXERCISE B Write the possessive form of each of the following words. Write your answers on the lines provided.

Example 1. my   *my*   [*My* is already possessive. It does not need an apostrophe and an *s*.]

6. everybody   __________ [Does *everybody* form its possessive by adding an apostrophe and an *s*?]

7. we   __________

8. no one   __________

9. they   __________

10. you   __________

EXERCISE C Write the possessive form of the word in parentheses after each of the following sentences. Write your answer on the lines provided.

Examples 1. Hand me   *my*   notebook, please. *(me)* [The possessive form of the personal pronoun *me* is *my*.]

    2. *The Smiths'* cart is blocking the aisle. *(The Smiths)* [The possessive form of the plural noun *Smiths* is formed by adding an apostrophe.]

11. Will ______________ artwork be displayed? *(everybody)* [Is *everybody* a word that forms its possessive by adding an apostrophe and an *s*?]

12. Don't forget ______________ wallet. *(you)* [Is *you* a word that forms its possessive by changing form?]

13. Isn't that ______________ cousin? *(Terry)*

14. Katie plays in a ______________ soccer league on Saturdays. *(women)*

15. Many of ______________ best songs have been recorded by other artists. *(the Beatles)*

16. Through the powerful binoculars, we could see several ______________ nests. *(eagles)*

17. Some people believe that a raccoon will wash ______________ food before it eats it. *(it)*

18. ______________ favorite movie will be showing this weekend. *(Maria)*

19. Have you finally found all of the ______________ toy mice? *(kitten)*

20. Randy said he would bring ______________ guitar to the picnic. *(he)*

Apostrophes B

Contractions

13r.	Use an apostrophe to show where letters, numerals, or words have been left out in a contraction.

A contraction is a shorter form of a word, a number, or a group of words. The apostrophe in a contraction shows where letters or numbers have been left out.

> **EXAMPLES** they + have = **they've**   here + is = **here's**
>
> can + not = **can't**   I + am = **I'm**
>
> of + the + clock = **o'clock**   1999 = **'99**

NOTE Do not confuse contractions and possessive personal pronouns. Possessive personal pronouns do not use apostrophes.

> **EXAMPLES** **It's** raining! [*It's* is a contraction for *It is*.]
>
> The rabbit wiggled **its** nose. [The word *its* is a possessive pronoun showing that the nose belongs to the rabbit.]

EXERCISE A Write the contraction for each of the following word groups. Write your answers on the lines provided.

Examples 1. he is ____*he's*____ [The contraction for *he is* is *he's*.]

2. 2004 ____*'04*____ [The contraction for 2004 is *'04*.]

1. should not __________ [Which letter should be replaced by an apostrophe in the contraction?]

2. 1960 __________ [Which numbers should be replaced by an apostrophe in the contraction?]

3. I have ______________

4. they are ______________

5. who is ______________

6. she will ______________

7. we would ______________

8. can not ______________

9. of the clock ______________

10. 2010 ______________

Plurals

13s.	Use an apostrophe and an *s* to form the plurals of letters, numerals, and symbols, and of words referred to as words.

> **EXAMPLES** How many *s*'s and *c*'s do you need in *unsuccessfully*? [The letters *s* and *c* are made plural by adding an apostrophe and an *s*.]

GO ON

> This address contains four *3*'**s**! [The numeral 3 is made plural by adding an apostrophe and an *s*.]
> Does the official name use *&*'**s** or *and*'**s**? [The symbol *&* is made plural by adding an apostrophe and an *s*. The word *and* is referred to as a word and also forms the plural by adding an apostrophe and an *s*.]

EXERCISE B Write the plural of the letter, numeral, symbol, or word given in parentheses after each of the following sentences. Write your answers on the lines provided.

Examples 1. Does anyone know the name for the _____*@'s*_____ in e-mail addresses? *(@)* [The plural of the symbol is formed by adding an apostrophe and an s.]

2. Try not to use so many _____*there's*_____ in your writing. *(there)* [The plural of the word *there* is formed by adding an apostrophe and an s.]

11. If you keep earning _______________, your grade point average will keep going up. *(A)* [How should the plural of a letter be formed?]

12. Did you remember to use _______________ in your math assignment? *(%)* [How should the plural of a symbol be formed?]

13. That child can say more _______________ in five minutes than anyone I've ever known. *(my)*

14. Put _______________ next to all the correct answers on your quiz. *(✓)*

15. The firefighter enjoyed the _______________ she got in response to her speech. *(hurray)*

16. Have you noticed that this pattern is made entirely of _______________? *(9)*

17. In journalism, three _______________ mean the end of the story. *(X)*

18. Darlene doesn't use many _______________ in her letters, so when she does, you know she means it! *(!)*

19. I've forgotten what these _______________ mean. *(π)*

20. If you use too many _______________ in your proposal, they might not accept it. *(maybe)*

Words with *ie* and *ei*

14a. Write *ie* when the sound is long *e*, except after *c*.

The long *e* sound is what you hear in words such as *brief, me, leaf.*

Write *ei* when the sound is not long *e*, especially when the sound is long *a*.

EXAMPLES	*i* before *e*	*ei* after *c*	*ei* pronounced *ay*
	bel**ie**f	dec**ei**ve	sl**ei**gh
	n**ie**ce	conc**ei**ted	**ei**ght
	f**ie**ld	c**ei**ling	w**ei**ght

TIP▶ This old rhyme may help you remember how to apply these spelling rules:

> *I* before *e*
> Except after *c*
> Or when sounded like *a*
> As in *neighbor* and *weigh.*

EXERCISE A In the following sentences, circle the word in parentheses that is spelled correctly.

Examples 1. The (**ceiling**, *cieling*) had brown spots where the roof had leaked during the storm. [The letters make the long *e* sound and come after a *c*. The correct spelling is *ceiling*.]

2. My (*nieghbors*, **neighbors**) have a swimming pool. [The letters are pronounced *ay*. The correct spelling is *neighbors*.]

1. Please save the (*reciept, receipt*) from the groceries. [Do the letters follow *c*? Are they pronounced with a long *a* sound?]

2. Did you (*recieve, receive*) the letter I sent you? [Do the letters follow *c*? Are they pronounced *ay*?]

3. The (*foreign, foriegn*) exchange student is from Greece.

4. Did you (*beleive, believe*) that story she told us?

5. If I win the spelling bee, I will (*acheive, achieve*) my goal.

6. Wild berries grow in the (*field, feild*) behind my house.

7. We had a (*breif, brief*) break between the two parts of the test.

8. I can't (*conceive, concieve*) of something being light years away.

9. My family goes on a (*sliegh, sleigh*) ride every winter.

10. Who will be the (*cheif, chief*) researcher on our team?

GO ON ▶

Developmental Language Skills

TIP Because there are so many exceptions to spelling rules, it is always a good idea to use a dictionary if you are unsure of how to spell a word.

EXERCISE B In the following sentences, circle the word in parentheses that is spelled correctly.

Examples 1. Have you ever been (*decieved,* *deceived*) by a magician's trick? [The letters make the long *e* sound and come after a *c*. The correct spelling is *deceived.*]

2. Three times a week, my mom lifts (*wieghts,* *weights*) at the gym. [The letters are pronounced *ay*. The correct spelling is *weights.*]

11. My aunt always tells me that I'm her favorite (*neice, niece*). [Do the letters follow *c*? Are they pronounced *ay*?]

12. I spent (*eight, ieght*) days at the beach this month. [Do the letters follow *c*? Are they pronounced with a long *a* sound?]

13. The homecoming queen will (*riegn, reign*) over the festivities.

14. We were held up at the crossing by a long (*frieght, freight*) train.

15. I had to (*forfeit, forfiet*) the match because my tennis partner was ill.

16. All the soccer players brought (*thier, their*) own soccer balls.

17. The jigsaw puzzle had over two thousand (*pieces, peices*)!

18. I was (*relieved, releived*) when the deadline was extended.

19. In December, our town always has a parade with real (*riendeer, reindeer*).

20. When the doctor measured my (*height, hieght*), I had grown two inches.

Prefixes and Suffixes

Prefixes

A *prefix* is a letter or a group of letters added to the beginning of a word to create a new word that has a different meaning.

14b. When adding a prefix to a word, do not change the spelling of the word itself.

> **EXAMPLES** un + able = un**able**   mis + spell = mis**spell** re + view = re**view**

EXERCISE A Add the prefix to the word for each of the following items. Write the new word on the line provided.

Example 1. un + necessary = ___*unnecessary*___ [Adding the prefix *un–* does not change the spelling of the word *necessary*.]

1. pre + caution = ______________ [Will adding a prefix change the spelling of the word *caution*?]

2. mis + understand = ______________

3. un + do = ______________

4. dis + like = ______________

5. re + wind = ______________

Suffixes

A *suffix* is a letter or a group of letters added at the end of a word to create a new word that has a different meaning.

14d. Drop the final silent *e* before adding a suffix that begins with a vowel.

A silent *e* is not pronounced when you say the word.

> **EXAMPLES** rake + ing = **rak**ing   love + able = **lov**able
> **EXCEPTIONS** Keep the silent *e* in words ending in *ce* and *ge* before adding a suffix beginning with *a* or *o*.
> peace + able = peac**eable**   outrage + ous = outrag**eous**

14e. Keep the final silent *e* before adding a suffix that begins with a consonant.

> **EXAMPLES** care + ful = **care**ful   nine + ty = **nine**ty

EXERCISE B Add the suffix to the word for each of the following items. Write the new word on the line provided.

Examples 1. hire + ing = ___*hiring*___ [The suffix *–ing* begins with a vowel, so the final silent *e* is dropped.]

2. safe + ty = ___*safety*___ [The suffix *–ty* begins with the consonant *t,* so the final silent *e* is kept.]

GO ON

6. remove + al = ______________

[Does the suffix

begin with a vowel

or a consonant?]

7. polite + ness = ______________

[Does the suffix

begin with a vowel

or a consonant?]

8. life + like = ______________

9. active + ity = ______________

10. trace + ing = ______________

11. pave + ment = ______________

12. hike + ing = ______________

13. love + ly = ______________

14. care + ful = ______________

15. taste + ed = ______________

14g. Double the final consonant before adding *–ing, –ed, –er,* or *–est* to a one-syllable word that ends in a single vowel followed by a single consonant.

    EXAMPLES sit + ing = si**tting**   hop + ed = ho**pped**

When a one-syllable word ends in two vowels followed by a single consonant, do not double the consonant before adding *–ing, –ed, –er,* or *–est.*

    EXAMPLES neat + est = nea**test**   keep + er = kee**per**

EXERCISE C Add the suffix to the word for each of the following items. Write the new word on the line provided.

Example 1. chop + ed = ___*chopped*___ [The one-syllable word *chop* ends in a vowel followed

    by a single consonant, so the *p* is doubled when adding the suffix *–ed.*]

16. cheat + er = ______________ [Does the word end in two vowels followed by a single

consonant?]

17. sleep + ing = ______________

18. dim + er = ______________

19. swim + ing = ______________

20. leak + ing = ______________

Plurals of Nouns

14h.   Follow these rules for spelling the plurals of nouns:

To form the plurals of most nouns, add *–s* to the end of the word.

SINGULAR	board	guy	igloo	solo
PLURAL	board**s**	guy**s**	igloo**s**	solo**s**

The plurals of some nouns are formed by adding *–es* to the end of the word.

SINGULAR	fax	peach	dish	tomato
PLURAL	fax**es**	peach**es**	dish**es**	tomato**es**

TIP Say the singular and plural forms of the word quietly to yourself. If the plural form has one more syllable than the singular, the plural is probably spelled by adding *–es* to the singular noun. A **syllable** is a word part that can be pronounced as one uninterrupted sound. (*Soft* has one syllable. *Softly* has two syllables [*soft • ly*]).

> **EXAMPLE**   The singular word *waltz* has one syllable. The plural word *waltzes* has two syllables: **waltz • es.** The plural word *waltzes* is formed by adding *–es* to the singular noun *waltz.*

EXERCISE A On the line provided, write the plural form of each of the following words.

Examples 1. pearl _____*pearls*_____ [The plural *pearls* has the same number of syllables as the singular *pearl.* The plural is formed by adding *–s.*]

2. fox _____*foxes*_____ [The plural *foxes* has one more syllable than the singular *fox.* The plural is formed by adding *–es.*]

1. flash ______________ [Does the plural form have the same number of syllables as the singular, or does the plural form have one more syllable than the singular?]

2. studio ______________ [Does the plural form have the same number of syllables as the singular, or does the plural form have one more syllable than the singular?]

3. birthday ______________

4. loss ______________

5. piano ______________

6. boy ______________

7. tax ______________

8. birch ______________

9. bottle ______________

10. cabinet ______________

GO ON

The plurals of some nouns are formed in different ways. Many words that end in *y* form the plural by changing the *y* to *i* before adding *–es*.

SINGULAR	cry	lady	enemy	apology
PLURAL	cr**ies**	lad**ies**	enem**ies**	apolog**ies**

Some nouns change in other ways to form the plural. A few nouns do not change at all to form the plural.

SINGULAR	mouse	ox	moose	scissors
PLURAL	m**ice**	ox**en**	moose	scissors

REMINDER If you are not sure how to spell the plural of a word, look the word up in a dictionary.

EXERCISE B On the line provided, write the plural form of each of the following words.

Examples 1. tooth ______*teeth*______ [The singular *tooth* changes to *teeth* to form the plural.]

2. knife ______*knives*______ [The *f* in *knife* changes to *v* and an *s* is added to form the plural.]

11. Chinese ____________ [Does the singular form change to form the plural, or is the plural form the same as the singular?]

12. pastry ____________ [Do any letters in the singular form change before *–es* is added to form the plural?]

13. woman ____________

14. trout ____________

15. lobby ____________

16. goose ____________

17. county ____________

18. salmon ____________

19. man ____________

20. blueberry ____________

Words Often Confused A

People often confuse the words in each of the following groups. Some of these words are *homonyms*—that is, they are pronounced the same. However, these words have different meanings and spellings. Other words in this section have the same or similar spellings yet have different meanings.

ALREADY [adverb] *at an earlier time*
We have **already** made our plans.

ALL READY [adjective] *all prepared; completely prepared*
We are **all ready** to leave for the parade.

ALTOGETHER [adverb] *entirely*
It was **altogether** too hot in the auditorium.

ALL TOGETHER [adjective] *in the same place*
We were **all together** at the cabin last weekend.
[adverb] *at the same time or place*
We sang **all together.**

BRAKE [noun] *a device to stop a machine*
The emergency **brake** needs to be fixed.

BREAK [verb] *to fracture; to shatter*
Don't **break** that glass!
[noun] *a fracture; an interruption; a rest*
I need a **break** before we start painting the next room.

EXERCISE A For each of the following sentences, circle the word or words in parentheses that will complete the sentence correctly.

Examples 1. I'm afraid he's going to (*brake,* *break*) that lamp. [The meaning is *to shatter.* The correct choice is *break.*]

2. We were (*already,* *all ready*) leaving when the phone rang. [The meaning is *at an earlier time.* The correct choice is *already.*]

1. The time we had to start out was (*altogether, all together*) too early for me. [Is the meaning *entirely* or *at the same time*?]

2. This one-speed bicycle has one hand (*brake, break*). [Is the meaning *a device to stop a machine* or *a rest*?]

3. We stayed there (*altogether, all together*) until it got dark.

4. After we finish the dishes, we'll take a (*brake, break*) before studying.

5. Are you sure you can be (*already, all ready*) to go by 5:00?

Developmental Language Skills   **125**

6. That roller coaster is *(altogether, all together)* too dangerous for a small child.

7. The *(brake, break)* on that go-cart is a special design.

8. Is it *(already, all ready)* time to go home?

9. Can we try to eat dinner *(altogether, all together)* tonight?

10. These newspapers are *(already, all ready)* to go in the recycling bin.

CHOOSE [verb, rhymes with *shoes*] *to select*
I'm hoping she'll **choose** me to play the princess in the play.

CHOSE [verb, past tense of *choose*, rhymes with *shows*]
I **chose** Nanette to assist me onstage.

CLOTHS [noun] *pieces of cloth*
We use those **cloths** for cleaning.

CLOTHES [noun] *wearing apparel*
My winter **clothes** are all in storage.

COARSE [adjective] *rough; crude; not fine*
This fabric is very **coarse.**

COURSE [noun] *a path of action; a series of studies*
Health is my favorite **course** this semester.
[also used in the expression *of course*]
Of **course,** I'll go with you.

EXERCISE B For each of the following sentences, circle the word in parentheses that will complete the sentence correctly.

Example 1. I need to find some *(cloths, clothes)* to wear at the beach. [The meaning is *wearing apparel.* The correct choice is *clothes.*]

11. The *(coarse, course)* I must take is clear. [Is the meaning *rough* or *a path of action*?]

12. Who *(choose, chose)* those wonderful decorations?

13. How many of these *(cloths, clothes)* will we piece together for the quilt?

14. I would *(choose, chose)* the red scooter over the silver one.

15. The *(coarse, course)* wood needs to be sanded before it's stained.

Words Often Confused B

People often confuse the words in each of the following groups. Some of these words are *homonyms*—that is, they are pronounced the same way. However, they have different meanings and spellings. Other words in this section have the same or similar spellings but have different meanings.

DESERT [noun, pronounced des′ • ert] *a dry, sandy region; a wilderness*
The saguaro cacti in the **desert** near Tucson are beautiful.

DESERT [verb, pronounced de • sert′] *to abandon; to leave*
Please don't **desert** me when we get to the party.

DESSERT [noun, pronounced des • sert′] *the final, sweet course of a meal*
We'll have fresh strawberries for **dessert.**

HEAR [verb] *to receive sounds through the ears*
How did you **hear** about the banquet?

HERE [adverb] *in this place*
The plates are **here** in this cabinet.

ITS [possessive form of *it*] *belonging to it*
This fan has outlived **its** usefulness.

IT'S [contraction of *it is* or *it has*]
It's a long way home from here.
It's been a wonderful day!

EXERCISE A For each of the following sentences, circle the word in parentheses that will complete the sentence correctly.

Example 1. We were hoping we had enough gas in the car to make it through the (*desert,*
dessert). [The meaning is *a dry, sandy region*. The correct choice is *desert*.]

1. (*Its, It's*) going to be a difficult test. [Is the word the possessive form of *it* or the contraction of *it is*?]

2. Could you bring the teakettle (*hear, here*)?

3. Tonight there won't be any (*desert, dessert*) with dinner.

4. Did the snake shed (*its, it's*) skin?

5. The connection was bad, and I couldn't (*hear, here*) her.

GO ON

LEAD [verb, rhymes with *need*] *to go first; to be a leader*
I could **lead** the way because I've been here before.

LED [verb, past tense of *lead*, rhymes with *red*] *went first; guided*
I **led** the tour group through the museum.

LEAD [noun, rhymes with *red*] *a heavy metal; graphite used in pencils*
This crystal has **lead** in it.
This is a No. 3 pencil, and the **lead** isn't dark enough.

LOOSE [adjective, rhymes with *goose*] *not tight*
This seat belt seems too **loose** to be safe.

LOSE [verb, rhymes with *shoes*] *to suffer loss*
How could you **lose** something that big?

PASSED [verb, past tense of *pass*] *went by*
She **passed** by me without looking up.

PAST [noun] *time that has gone by*
That's all in the **past** now.
[preposition] *beyond*
We drove slowly **past** her house.
[adjective] *ended*
The **past** month has been very quiet.

EXERCISE B For each of the following sentences, circle the word in parentheses that completes the sentence correctly.

Example **1.** Rene will now (*lead*, *led*) us in two verses of "Amazing Grace." [The meaning is *to go first; to be a leader*. The correct choice is *lead*.]

6. He said your mom's car (*passed*, *past*) him on the way to school. [Is the meaning *went by* or *time that has gone by*?]

7. If the bolt is (*loose*, *lose*), tighten it with this wrench.

8. My grandmother loves talking about the (*passed*, *past*).

9. She (*lead*, *led*) our scout troop for about three years.

10. Do you think our team will win or (*loose*, *lose*) the next game?

Words Often Confused C

People often confuse the words in each of the following groups. Some of these words are *homonyms*—that is, they are pronounced the same way. However, they have different meanings and spellings. Other words in this section have the same or similar spellings but have different meanings.

PEACE [noun] *quiet; order; security*
The **peace** and quiet in the little valley was soothing.

PIECE [noun] *a part of something*
Save me a **piece** of that meatloaf.

THEIR [possessive form of *they*] *belonging to them*
Their car has been at the mechanic's for two weeks.

THERE [adverb] *at or to that place*
I'll take my lunch over **there.**
[also used to begin a sentence]
There might be some left.

THEY'RE [contraction of *they are*]
Hurry, **they're** going to catch up!

EXERCISE A For each of the following sentences, circle the word in parentheses that will complete the sentence correctly.

Example 1. Could you cut me a (*peace,* *piece*) of that ribbon? [The meaning is *a part of something.*
The correct choice is *piece.*]

1. The teacher graded (*their, there, they're*) papers during class. [Is the meaning *belonging to them* or *at that place* or the contraction of *they are*?]

2. (*Their, There, They're*) going to be very excited when they hear the news.

3. Are you going (*their, there, they're*) to visit relatives?

4. (*Their, There, They're*) visit cheered me up.

5. Would you like a (*peace, piece*) of bread with that?

GO ON

TO [preposition] *in the direction of; toward*
We drove **to** my friend's house.

TOO [adverb] *also; more than enough*
He brought me some roses, **too.**
Is the music **too** loud?

TWO [adjective or noun] *one plus one*
They bought **two** red chairs.

WEAK [adjective] *feeble; not strong*
I felt **weak** the whole time I had the flu.

WEEK [noun] *seven days*
This **week** has gone by slowly.

WHO'S [contraction of *who is* or *who has*]
Who's going to count the laps in the race?
Who's been using my computer?

WHOSE [possessive form of *who*] *belonging to whom*
Whose drawing won first place?

YOUR [possessive form of *you*] *belonging to you*
Your painting is beautiful!

YOU'RE [contraction of *you are*]
I'm glad **you're** here.

EXERCISE B For each of the following sentences, circle the word in parentheses that will complete the sentence correctly.

Example 1. I'll take the books back (*to*, *too*, *two*) the library. [The meaning is *in the direction of; toward*. The correct choice is *to*.]

6. Are you enjoying (*your*, *you're*) mountain bike? [Is the meaning *belonging to you* or the contraction of *you are?*]

7. I feel (*to*, *too*, *two*) sleepy to finish reading the book tonight.

8. The (*weak*, *week*) light from the lamp barely lit the room.

9. (*Who's*, *Whose*) the girl with the red hair?

10. (*Your*, *You're*) such a good friend!

Common Errors Review

Common Usage Errors

Be sure that you proofread each writing assignment before you turn it in. Errors in your writing can confuse and distract your readers. In fact, readers may form a poor impression of a writer who makes careless errors. Look for errors, especially in the following areas:

Do subjects and verbs agree?   Are modifiers in the correct form?
Do pronouns and antecedents agree?   Are modifiers placed correctly?
Are verb forms and tenses correct?   Is usage appropriate for audience and purpose?

After you make corrections or changes, read your writing again. Sometimes a change you make will create a new problem in another part of your writing.

The two exercises that follow will help you recognize and correct common errors in usage and mechanics.

EXERCISE A The following items contain common errors in usage. Review the list of problem areas above and correct the errors. Use proofreading marks to make your corrections.

Examples 1. At my school, all students is required to participate in a community service project in the sixth grade. [The plural subject *students* needs the plural verb *are*, not the singular verb *is*. The phrase *in the sixth grade* should be moved closer to *students*, the word it modifies.]

2. The year before last, the food drive was successfully, so students vote to hold a food drive again last year. [The linking verb *was* should be followed by the adjective *successful*, not the adverb *successfully*. The sentence is in the past tense, so the verb form should be *voted*, not the present tense *vote*.]

1. In September, class representatives in the cafeteria met and form committees. [Are modifiers placed correctly? Are verb tenses consistent?]

2. Than, everyone chose their job. [Are any words misused? Do pronouns and antecedents agree?]

3. One group collects bags and boxes, and several asked his or her parents to help with transportation.

4. During October, the journalism teacher learned us how to write press releases, and we sended the press releases to the newspapers and radio stations.

5. We sat up an information booth in the hallway and had hung posters in the neighborhood.

6. Working with teachers, maps were drew by one group.

7. On a sunny Saturday morning, we all meet in the parking lot and got their assignments.

GO ON

8. Parents had went with students to knock on doors and except donations of canned food.

9. Some neighbors had already brung his donations to the school.

10. We could of collected more, but there wasn't no more room in the boxes.

Common Mechanics Errors

When you write, always check your capitalization, punctuation, and spelling. Use a dictionary if you are not sure of a spelling or a word division. Make sure you haven't confused two words that sound alike but are spelled differently. These details make a big difference in your writing! Look for errors in the following areas, too:

Does every sentence begin with a capital letter?
Are all proper nouns capitalized?
Does every sentence end with an appropriate end mark?
Have you placed commas where they are needed?
Are direct quotations and titles capitalized and punctuated correctly?
Are words spelled and divided correctly?

EXERCISE B The following paragraph contains mistakes in mechanics. Correct the errors in capitalization, punctuation, and spelling. Use proofreading marks to make your corrections.

Example 1. At exactly 11:30 next saturday morning mayor Johnson will officially open the new

youth center. [The hour and the minutes in *11:30* should be separated with a colon.

Saturday should be capitalized because it is the name of a day of the week. A comma

should separate the two introductory prepositional phrases from the main sentence. The

title *Mayor* should be capitalized because it comes before the person's name.]

11. An article in the Morning News said that the center will be open every day except monday.

[Are titles underlined? Are days of the week capitalized?]

12. According to the article in the Newspaper the center will be named the lillian carter youth

center

13. The reporter wrote Everyone agrees that mrs. Carter a well known volunteer in the neighbor-

hood deserves the honor.

14. After we skate we can play volleyball maybe we can watch a movie to.

15. Oops Id better get off the phone now its all ready time to leave for the ceremony